# But Did You Die?

A collection of humorous essays by

A Bunch of Know-It-Alls

# Contents

# INTRODUCTION

When I gave birth for the first time twelve years ago, I was more than a little terrified. I felt like I received more care instructions when I purchased a goldfish than when I took my tiny baby home from the hospital. I had shelves and shelves of parenting books, but none of them offered me real-world advice. One told me to "introduce" my baby to our home and explain to him what happens in each room. Telling my infant, "This is the kitchen. This is where we get our eat-on at," seemed like a total waste of time. I didn't know if I should sleep train or let him cry it out. Should I swaddle him? How tight was too tight? Why did he cry so much? What did he want? So, I turned to the experts in my life: my grandmother, who was the mother of four, and my own mother. The first gift my grandmother gave my child was a wheeled walker that she bought for an exorbitant price from her neighbor's garage sale. "Grandma, I'm pretty sure those are banned," I told her. "They're quite dangerous. Also, your neighbor completely overcharged you."

Grandma replied, "Oh, they're not so bad. Your Uncle Carl only fell down the basement stairs twice in his."

My mother was also a wealth of terrible advice. The first time I took my baby to the pool I slathered him in 1000 SPF sunblock, twenty-six layers of sun-repellent clothing, and a hat with a brim bigger than his whole body.

My mother frowned. "When you were a baby, I just rolled you under my beach chair."

"Excuse me?" I said.

"I put a towel down. You weren't on the ground or anything," she said, all huffy—like that was the problem.

"You rolled me under your beach chair? How old was I?"

"Hmm, three months, or so? It was a good place for you. Nice and shady. Because I don't think sunblock is good for babies," she said. "We never put sunblock on you kids."

"Yes, Mom, I know," I replied. "That's why I have to go to the dermatologist every year and have her literally check my asshole for skin cancer. I've had several suspicious moles removed and I have permanent skin damage from the sun."

"Okay, but did you die?" she asked.

That was my mother's response to everything when I questioned her parenting choices. Car seats didn't even exist when I was a baby and seat belts were a suggestion until I was in college. I rode my bike willy-nilly without a helmet. I drank soda as an infant and chewed on toys painted with lead paint. Everybody around me smoked. I've never worn a life jacket on a boat.

I don't baby my kids, but compared to the way I was raised, my kids are being raised in a cushion of bubble wrap. I *think* I'm doing a good job raising them, but who knows? Luckily, now I have the parents (and even a few opinionated non-breeders) of the Internet to give me advice. I don't follow it all, but it's nice to pick and choose and make sure that at least I'm screwing up my kids in the same way everyone else is. I'm sure in twenty years my children will be horrified by all the terrible things I did and my response will be, "But did you die?"

—Jen Mann

# A Primer on Handling Childhood Pet Deaths
## By Janel Mills
### *649.133: Girls, the Care and Maintenance Of,*

Well, the day you've been simultaneously daydreaming about and dreading for the last few years has finally arrived: your child's pet is dead. It's an important milestone in your parenting career, and make no mistake—the fuck-up factor on this one is pretty high. If you don't get this one right, your actions will be mentioned at every single Thanksgiving and probably several Buzzfeed-esque compilations of shitty parenting stories ad infinitum.

Here's a few tips and tricks I learned when my daughter's beloved hamster, Brownie Pancakes, kicked the bucket last summer after two and a half excruciating years.

**Keep your celebrations private.** I am a total animal nut. I've had almost every kind of pet you can own, and I spend most of my time at parties trying to convince the hosts' cats to like me. However, if I had to rank the happiest days of my life, they would be (in this order):

- The birth of my children
- My wedding day
- The day that fucking hamster bought the teeny tiny farm

But I couldn't show that emotion at home, because my kids, for some inexplicable reason, loved Brownie Pancakes. Despite the fact that her hobbies were eating, sleeping all day long, biting the person holding her, and escaping from her cage and throwing the entire household into full-blown WTF mode, my daughter still made that thing a birthday card and convinced everyone in her third-grade class to sign the card. So please, keep your double crane kicks and fist pumps confined to someplace your kids can't see or hear you.

**Make sure it's *really* dead.** With some pets, it's pretty obvious they've gone to that deluxe litter box in the sky. If you wake up and your bird is lying on the bottom of the cage, it's pretty safe to assume it's done. Fish generally don't sleep sideways at the top of the tank. But with other pets, it's not so easy. During Brownie Pancakes's final days, I would stare at that hamster for at least a full minute sometimes to see if it was still breathing, and just when I was ready to crack open the champagne, BOOM—it breathed. One morning, though, I stared at that thing for like five minutes and felt pretty confident this was the real deal. No breathing, no moving. But then later that day, as I was helping my kids draw pictures for the funeral, my husband looked at me and quietly said, "Are you *sure* it's dead?" Which is an important question to ask, because I don't know about you, but I'm not trying to start a Pet Sematary in my backyard. I saw that movie; it did not end well for anybody involved. Plus, can you imagine how many points you'd lose if you (or, let's be real, the designated person in your life who touches dead things because LOL NO) put your kid's pet into the funeral shoebox and *it fucking comes back to life?!* That is *no bueno* on so many levels. So trust me, poke it with a stick, hold a miniature mirror under its nose, do whatever you have to do to make sure it's not just merely dead, but really most sincerely dead.

**Don't get creative.** This is not the time to involve Pinterest in your decision-making. Unless you really hated that ferret and already have an entire secret board dedicated to pet funerals, then by all means, feel free to look into a little bit of therapy for yourself because you might have a few things you need to work out. On the same note, don't make this the moment you decide to educate your kids about "going green" by dumping their pet directly into the ground because it's more biodegradable (i.e., you're cheap and hated that fucking parakeet anyways), or go back to your art school days and try something avant-garde and "meaningful." Translation: don't try flushing the hamster down the toilet because you think it makes some kind of bold statement about the the fleetingness of life or some goofy shit like that. Keep it boring and traditional. Trust me, the kids will find a way to make it interesting enough without you adding to the experience.

**Be respectful of the dead**. Try not to focus on all the things that sucked about the pet that passed when talking to your kids. Brownie Pancakes was the worst pet on the face of the Earth, but just like you don't read off all the charges on Aunt Dora's rap sheet at her funeral wake, don't begin reminding the household how much you disliked getting up at 2 a.m. to move Brownie Pancakes's cage because hamsters are nocturnal, *did you know that*? I sure didn't when I agreed to get one for my daughter, who is the lightest sleeper in the history of light sleepers. Try to focus on the more pleasant things about the pet. For example, Brownie Pancakes liked to stuff food in her cheeks, and she almost always ran to the same bedroom closet when she escaped. There. That's, like, two whole positive things about that hamster. Beer me.

**Hold an actual ceremony.** This is not negotiable. If you don't live in the suburbs, find someone with a small patch of land that will let you bury your dead animal. At the very least, hold a memorial service, and you'd better goddamn get yourself an enormous picture of that gecko and have it on display while you share your precious memories of him. You have to hold a proper funeral, not because it's the right thing to do or the kids need "closure," but because it will be the cutest, saddest, funniest thing you will experience as a family. It's worth the animal dying for the memory of the event you're about to witness. It's nice because in a way, it serves as a trial run for any future funerals you may decide to attend with your children (or not, depending on how this thing goes).

Make sure you adhere to all the trappings of a funeral. My appointed dead-things-toucher and husband, for example, went all *Deadwood* and built a tiny wooden coffin for Brownie Pancakes. After he dug the hole in the spot behind our garage that serves as our animal graveyard, the kids and I solemnly walked through the backyard with Brownie Pancakes's casket in hand. My oldest daughter, the bereaved owner, was appropriately solemn. My youngest daughter was crying so hard she was ready to throw herself on the coffin and be dragged off by family members who know she's all drama, and were 100 percent ready for her to pull something like this and arranged themselves around her accordingly. My middle daughter, however, was mostly just pissed she had to pause her video game to go talk about feelings.

5

"Let's all go around and say something nice about Brownie Pancakes."

"Brownie Pancakes was a really good hamster. I loved her a lot, and I'm really going to miss her."

"I JUST REALLY MISS BROWNIEEEEEEEEEEEEEEEEE!"

"Surrey, you never even held Brownie Pancakes and said she was mean because she bit you once."

"Are we done yet? Can I go back inside?"

"No, Bella, we're not done telling nice stories about Brownie."

"But I am! I need to get back and beat Chef Pepper Jack!"

"WHY DID BROWNIE HAVE TO DIE????????"

"Mom, is this the part where we sprinkle the dirt on the coffin?"

"Yeah, you can…Surrey! You're going to fall in—"

"Mom, SHE'S STEPPING ON MY HAMSTER'S COFFIN!"

"Is Brownie Pancakes going to come back to life? Is she a zombie now?"

"What?! No, Brownie Pancakes is dead. She's not ever coming back to life. She's staying dead forever."

Then everyone starts crying and you go back into the house, and you congratulate yourself on building more precious memories with your children.

**Keep the pet's memory alive.** Just like with people, make sure you do something that helps keep the memory of your beloved family member alive in everyone's mind. There's lots of ways you can do that—a special keepsake album, a little statue in the backyard where your fantastic funeral service was held, maybe a Christmas ornament. I chose to honor Brownie Pancakes by putting her empty cage in the back of my minivan, then driving around town for months so my kids could hear the rattle of her cage door whenever we hit a bump and be reminded of Brownie Pancakes's demise. I meant to donate her cage and the rest of her unused supplies to our local animal shelter, but you know how that goes—it's a few months before you finally get tired of piling groceries around your old crap and finally turn your shit in. As it turns out, turning your main mode of transportation to school and family functions into a hearse will definitely keep your pet's memory alive. Removing the cage every once in a while to make room for bigger items and leaving it on the back porch, next to the door you use to go in and out of your house every day, can also give a big boost to the constant questions about whether or not Brownie Pancakes is in heaven or if she is, again, going to come back to life at night and start living in her cage again.

So, shout-out to all the moms and dads out there keeping a hopeful, disdainful watch over those unwanted critters. Your day will come, I promise you. Every time you have to clean those cages or endure another bite from that thing, just remember: one day, you'll be settling arguments about whose turn it is to play Skylanders over its grave.

And then promptly driving to PetSmart to purchase another animal, because that is the Childhood Pet Circle of Life. *Naaaaaaazipenya*, y'all.

*JANEL MILLS is the librarian/thug behind the blog 649.133: Girls, the Care and Maintenance Of, where she writes about raising a princess, a wild child, and the sassiest redhead on Earth using as many curse words as possible. Janel was a contributor to NickMom, and is also a contributor to several wildly successful anthologies including the I Just Want to Pee Alone series. She's also been featured on The Mighty, Scary Mommy, and The Huffington Post. You can find her on Facebook or on all the other things at @649point133. When not blogging or librarian-ing, she keeps busy raising three beautiful little girls with her beardedly gifted husband in the wilds of metro Detroit.*

# Set the Bar Low: A Guide to Perfect Parenting
## By Meredith Gordon
### *Bad Sandy*

As a general practice, I like to learn the hard way. If something can be done easily, I like to avoid that. Shortcuts are not for me. I'm a long-cut kind of a gal. So when I gave birth to my son I looked into his clear-blue-why-couldn't-they-have-stayed-blue eyes and vowed to be the perfect mother. "I'm going to do right by you, little man," I said in a fit of hormonal delusion, not knowing when it comes to parenting, not raising a serial killer should be one's only goal. In a world of attachment parents, stay-at-home moms, working moms, organic moms, nursing moms, nursing moms who don't believe in nursing moms, I've learned the hard way I'm a set-the-bar-low kind of mom. Goals and perfection are for other moms. Getting by is for people like me.

Learning to set the bar low came to me later in life. I had to learn the hard way. For example, in a fit of delusion I once trained for a marathon. If you know anything about marathons, you know they involve running for 26.2 miles, which is ridiculous for anyone to attempt because Henry Ford invented cars. But I was naïve and told friends a time in which I wanted to complete the race. "Under four hours," I said smugly to friends and family. Four hours and one minute later, I finished the race only to feel like an utter disappointment for not achieving my under-four-hours goal. Had I simply said, "I hope to finish before the beginning of the next century," I would have been a local hero.

Surely, we've all had the gut-wrenching experience of boasting about our new health kick to friends. A day later, a friend catches you in your car at school pickup downing French fries and you're automatically branded a quitter. Had you said you were trying to lose half a pound, "sometime over the next year," no one would bat an eyelash. In fact, that same friend might have even celebrated your resolve and would have lauded you an overachiever. But now, because of your publicly stated high goals, you'll always be known as the car binger who couldn't last a day on her diet.

When I had my first child, a boy, I hadn't quite gotten the lesson. I was still determined to do a good job. A really, really good job. I wanted to make up for my past career foibles and all those awful boyfriends I had dated before I met the one. I wanted to finally get something right. I wanted to be a perfect mother.

And if there's one thing I knew, it was that perfect mothers breastfed their children. So I decided, through extensive research (reading one article I Googled), that the mouths of my children would never, ever touch formula. I breastfed like it was an Olympic sport and I wanted to win the gold. The problem was, my son was one of those distracted little fellows who needed low lighting and a quiet environment to nurse. So every four hours, I'd sequester myself in a dark room, close the door, and feed my kid. I'd had dates in less romantic settings, but I was determined never to formula feed my precious baby. And that fact I'd tell to anyone who would listen.

By the time I weaned him on his first birthday, my breasts and I were exhausted. Not only had I not given my son formula, I hadn't given him bottles. His entire nourishment relied on me and my sleep-deprived boobs. So on his first birthday I gave him a kiss on the check and proclaimed it was time for him to start seeing other people. I felt guilty for being so happy that I was free of the responsibility, and time constraints, of breastfeeding. But the truth is, I was happy and relieved. I wish I had taken note and set the bar low then and there, but I was still trying to take the road longest traveled. I still wanted to get parenting right.

So I decided my son would never ever have baby food that wasn't homemade. For a person whose top 200 skills do not include cooking, this was ambitious. And because I had hired a babysitter who once said, "Mix all baby food with sweet potatoes," I mixed everything with sweet potatoes. So I'd puree strawberries and add sweet potatoes. I'd mash up a banana and add sweet potatoes. Applesauce? Yup, sweet potatoes. It never occurred to me I couldn't be paid to eat a sweet potato, much less a sweet potato mixed with strawberry (good god!) or a sweet potato mixed with banana (hold my hair while I puke, please).

A few days into solids, my son took one look at his sweet-potato-of-the-day combo and hurled it across the room, leaving my living room walls looking like they were being prepped for a Thanksgiving sequel to *The Shining*. To this day he looks at sweet potatoes and winces. So do I.

When my son was three I began looking at preschools, which was apparently three years and nine months late to look at Los Angeles's finest preschools. I had no idea that from the first thumbs-up on a pregnancy test, I was supposed to be investigating and researching preschools. Other mom friends would remind me studies have proven kids who go to preschool are some percent I've forgotten less likely to grow up to commit crimes and go to jail. If my kid didn't get into preschool, he might in fact become a serial killer. I had to act fast. I had to make up for lost time. I had to get him in.

So I approached finding a preschool for my son like it was really me who was getting in. I became on expert on teaching philosophies and could outline the difference between a progressive school, a development teaching philosophy, the Montessori theory, and the Reggio Emilia philosophy, which my husband still to this day refers to as "The Regis and Kelly method."

I made spreadsheets, bookmarked websites, kept an updated calendar of application schedules, and curated lists of contacts who might help us get our son into our top choice preschools. I networked, I charmed, and I took Mommy & Me classes at each of our top-choice preschools to maximize sucking up. If it were up to my kid, he would have chosen our safety preschool. He seemed happiest at the backup. But getting into preschool wasn't about joy or comfort. It was about getting my three-year-old into college someday and keeping him from becoming a criminal. He'd have a lifetime to do things he loved. Preschool was about setting him on the right path and ensuring his future.

But it wasn't until I had my second child and got my ass kicked by postpartum that I realized my tombstone would never read, "Here lies Meredith, she breastfed exclusively. She made her children's baby food entirely from scratch. And her children studied finger painting and hair pulling at the finest institutions." Two days after having my daughter, it became clear to me something was awry. I was thrilled to have her, but postpartum kept me numb. The idea of breastfeeding as intensely as I had with my son had me feeling trapped.

And so I didn't.

Whereas my son never had a bottle, my daughter never had a boob. She had formula. And she lived through it. I did too. In fact, I did better than live through it. I loved it. I loved not being solely responsible for her health and well-being. I loved not having to do everything for her. I loved sharing the load. I loved, as it turns out, setting the bar low.

I quickly became a low expectations addict. I threw out my baby food maker and bought the store-bought jars I'd been sure would kill my first child. I stopped worrying about whether or not my kid was in *the* preschool and became happy with my son's preschool, which boasted clean floors and only a few kids who bit my son regularly. The kids were happy, so why did I need to make things more difficult than they needed to be? The answer was, I didn't. My kids are getting bigger. My son is nine and the little girl is six and in kindergarten. I've been setting the bar low for six years now and I've pretty much gotten the hang of it. I often forget to do my kids' laundry before they run out of underwear and have to tell them, "Turn it inside out. It's clean on the other side." I rarely remember to make dinner until dinnertime and am only able to cover that fact by shouting, "It's breakfast for dinner night. Yippee!" as a justification for why I'm pouring bowls of cereal for dinner.

I always have to pay for overnight shipping because I can't for the life of me remember to order all those birthday presents for the never-ending season of kids' parties. I stopped volunteering at school and can only name half the kids in my kids' classes. I let my kids watch *Pitch Perfect* despite the continued sexual innuendos I pray went over their heads. And my daughter was playing a very intense game of "Family" at school and used the words *go, fuck,* and *yourself,* in the game because, "That's how my Mommy talks."

But despite my kids' store-bought baby food, third-tier preschool, and Cheerios for dinner, neither has, to date, become a serial killer. And everyone knows that if your kids don't grow up to be serial killers you've done a good job raising them, even if you set the bar low and can't remember to make dinner.

*MEREDITH GORDON is the author behind the side-splitting humor blog* Bad Sandy. *She is known for her gracious letters to Gwyneth Paltrow, her parenting advice from Kim Kardashian written in first-person Kim, and her spot-on commentary on her husband's inability to wash all the dishes. She is currently in preproduction on her first television show* Porn Moms *(Endemol, USA), a title that continues to make her mother proud. Meredith lives in Los Angeles where she is raising her husband and two children.*

# Talk Like an Adult
## By Joel Ryan
### *The Glad Stork*

"Talk like an adult," I said.

My daughter was whining at the dinner table and it just came out. "Talk like an adult." An adult? But she was only four years old.

Flashback to when she was a baby. A relative, who shall remain nameless, was holding her. Looking down with a clown-like face of jubilation, the relative said, in a twangy voice, "Her's gettin' some toofins! Yes her is. Yes her is!"

*Her's not gonna understand her's pronouns,* I thought.

In that moment, I decided to never talk to my kids in baby talk. I would always speak like an adult to them. Dress for the job you want, not the one you have, so to speak. Just like if you let your kid watch *Peppa Pig* for a couple weeks straight they develop a slight British accent and a dislike of bacon, I figured if I spoke to my kids in properly enunciated, un-simplified ways, they would develop full vocabularies and the ability to express nuanced thoughts beyond, "Her's gettin' some toofins!"

So my advice to new parents is this: avoid baby talk and introduce advanced concepts earlier than you think is possible. Kids can stretch intellectually. The results can be amazing, inspiring, and sometimes hilarious.

When my daughter was eighteen months old, I received a phone call from daycare. Worried she had become a biter—what with her's toofins and whatnot—I anxiously answered. The daycare teacher was laughing so hard she could barely speak. She explained my daughter had tottered over to her, tugged on her leg, looked up, and said, "I am con-sti-pated. I need stool softener."

But every kid develops differently. I once overheard several parents at a restaurant taking turns bragging about their kids. The bragging was punctuated by an old man with them grumbling, "Ugh, tell me what they're doing when they're eighteen." So perhaps this is just the way my daughter is, but I like to think her verbal precociousness began with the "no baby talk" mandate.

In the film *Hook*, Robin Williams's character gets upset with his son Jack and sneers, "When will you stop acting like a child?!" To which Jack replies, "But I am a child."

Speaking to your kids like adults certainly encourages proper enunciation, pronunciation, and a full vocabulary, but perhaps it takes some of the magic out of childhood. Grown-up language and grown-up reasoning go hand in hand. It's tough to draw the line.

My daughter once asked, "Daddy, do you believe in magic?"

I paused, considering the age-appropriate response, and answered, "Magic isn't real. If magic was real, it would be called science."

She fired back, "That's not true. Santa is magic and he is real. You don't know. You are wrong!"

With her adamant response, dripping with condescension, I was just moments away from destroying her innocence. I felt like if I just said, "Come on, think about it," several times in a row she would have figured out the whole Santa thing. Just a few days earlier she inspected a soccer ball she received from the Jolly Old Elf. "Made in China? HOW DID SANTA GET THIS IF IT WAS MADE IN CHINA?"

"Come on, think about it."

When my daughter was four she was upset about a cheap plastic toy that broke beyond repair. Without thinking I quipped, "Everything crumbles eventually. In billions of years the sun will expand and consume the Earth. But don't worry, we'll all be dead by then." Father of the year. Surprisingly she took this grim reality in stride. "Okay, can we watch TV?" Sure thing.

Perhaps this amount of mature directness leads to premature melancholy and jadedness. My daughter once asked how my day was. I told her, "Not bad. Lots of meetings and deadlines." Appalled at what she thought she had heard, she said, "DEAD LIONS?!"

Kids are sponges. They soak up your attitude, language, and worldviews, whether you like it or not. Speaking to your kids like they're adults gives you a glimpse into what you are really like, as if you're looking into a mirror of your subconsciousness.

I asked my daughter one Monday morning when she was three, "How was your weekend, buddy?" She said, "It was… good. It was just… too busy." My three-year-old was complaining about her busy weekend like an old hen chitchatting around the office water cooler.

Once I took her to the dentist with me. While I was getting my teeth cleaned, she sat nearby, talking with the hygienist about this and that, the weather, traffic… you know, kid stuff. A car commercial came on the TV. My daughter said, "Commercials just try to brainwash you into buying things you don't need." It was like hearing a tiny version of myself. The hygienist was shocked, but also slightly more enlightened about the pervasiveness of consumerist culture, I'd like to imagine.

I didn't just promote sophisticated language with my kids, I also encouraged them to speak up, in polite and appropriate ways of course. But no matter the kid, the social filter is always the same: nonexistent. This leads to some entertaining exchanges. Here is a partial list of some of the things my daughter has said to waiters:

- Are you going to lie to try to get us to buy things?
- How do you eat if you're always here during dinnertime?
- If this place is so fancy, how come you don't have any chandeliers?

That last one was met with the most inspirational thing I've ever heard a waiter say, "You don't have to *look* fancy to *be* fancy."

My daughter had a large vocabulary at a young age and spoke with eloquence and sophistication. Before she was two she had developed such a reputation at our local pharmacy that when we'd fill a prescription, the pharmacist would get people from the back to come check out "the amazing talking baby."

My son, on the other hand, was not quite as loquacious, as younger siblings can often be. But he shared her blunt directness and willingness to speak his mind. He had an unusually dry sarcastic wit that was well beyond his years. He was like a tiny Yogi Berra. I never spoke to him in baby talk either, and he began experimenting with the art of language at an early age, creating an alternative collection of quips and phrases that became famous among our family and friends.

Here are a few of his witticisms, all from his third year:

- bacon sauce = grease
- girl polish = lotion
- marker juice = paint
- a special Cajun = a special occasion
- hee-haw! = hi-yah! (karate kick exclamation)
- hole hair = curly hair
- Papa John cheese = parmesan cheese
- cooking scraper = spatula
- chocolate jello = pudding
- sun cream = sunscreen
- night night bugs = lightning bugs
- micro oven = microwave
- night light sword = lightsaber
- sea shark = whale
- crumble bread = cornbread

When he was four, I brought him along to a work function. My boss leaned down to talk to him. She said in a bubbly voice, "Oh my. You are so cute. How old are you, little guy?"

"Four."

"And when do you turn five?"

He rolled his eyes. "After four."

Once I asked him if he'd like a frozen pizza. He said, "No, thanks. I'd like it warm."

The other day I gave him a bite of cotton-candy-flavored yogurt. "What does this taste like?" He took a bite, and looking at me like I was an idiot, he said, "Yogurt."

*Ugh, I'm raising the personification of an Abbott and Costello routine*, I thought.

Language is an important part of development. Not just our children's development, but our own as well. As parents we need to be mindful of the way we communicate to our kids, because it will become the foundation for how they speak to each other and to other adults. I decided I'd rather have my kid become a dental hygienist who espouses the harmful aspects of consumerism than one who says, "Is her gettin' some toofins?"

But it's a balance. They're only kids once. So for now, in my house, the magic of Santa remains and we call grease "bacon sauce."

"Talk like an adult? But I'm just a kid," she said.

"You're right; you're right. You can talk like a kid."

A smile crept onto her face. "Poop," she said. And we all giggled.

*JOEL RYAN is not a stork; he just pretends to be one on the Internet, creating absurd content as* The Glad Stork *about parenting, marriage, cubicle life, rap music, and more. In real life, he is a husband, father, cubicle dweller, writer, designer, photographer, humorist, children's book author, illustrator, and idiot. He can be found on* Facebook, Instagram, Twitter, *and* thegladstork.com.

# When People Make Plans, God Laughs: Shit Happens
## By Jen Simon

Our Flight From Hell began in the usual way our flights began—with my husband complaining about how much I packed.

"Why would we possibly need this much stuff? Did you even leave anything at home?" Matt, my husband, huffed as we boarded the plane.

"Stop exaggerating. Besides," I replied "we don't know what we're going to need."

"Yeah, but I'm the one who has to carry it all," he grumbled as he lugged the bags behind him.

I didn't know why he was so cranky. After all, I had only packed the absolute necessities for our five-day trip to visit my parents. In addition to our checked bag, we had two carry-on bags, my purse, and a tote I used as a diaper bag. Oh yeah, and our two-and-a-half-year-old son, Noah.

The contents of my tote bag included: diapers and wipes; a portable changing pad; a flip book of alphabet flash cards; a blank sketchpad; a box of crayons; a small musical toy we jokingly called his iPod; his lovey; his favorite stuffed animal (a black-and-white cat); three Matchbox cars; one small fire engine; a handful of mini figurines; a blanket; hand sanitizer; his water bottle; a burp cloth; four books; a mini pack of tissues; a DVD player; three DVDs; and a pair of children's headphones. Because the flight clocked in at just over two whole hours, I also packed two peanut butter and jelly sandwiches; three granola bars; three fruit leathers; snack bags of almonds, cashews, raisins, and Cheerios; and an organic lollipop from Trader Joe's (for a bribe). And lastly (and most importantly) an extra shirt, pair of pants, and pair of socks for Noah.

My bag was crammed so full of stuff that even if I had been able to pull the stick out of my ass, I wouldn't have had anywhere to put it.

I didn't take nearly as much care packing my purse. After all, I had my Xanax—that was enough, right?

I didn't realize I was every new(ish) crunchy mother cliché. But at the time, none of it felt silly—it felt necessary. Important, even. *People make plans and God laughs*, my mom had told me on more than one occasion. I didn't know if I believed in God, but I knew I believed in anxiety. If I planned for eventualities, it quieted the panic in my mind. Planning made me feel like I had control over an uncontrollable situation. Hahahahahahaha.

While we had flown with Noah before, it was our first flight where he was old enough to require his own ticket. I luxuriated in the three-seat row that belonged to just our family. Our seclusion turned out to be a *very* good thing.

We were only a few minutes into our flight—the "fasten seat belt" light wasn't even off yet—when Noah said his stomach hurt.

"Do you want a sandwich? Some nuts? Cheerios?" As a Jewish mother, I was morally obligated to offer him food. He shook his head and leaned against me.

"Why don't you distract him with some books?" I suggested.

While Matt was fumbling with the tote, Noah complained again.

"Mommy, my tummy hurts."

The words were barely out of his mouth before they were followed by a stream of vomit. Matt jerked up from the tote, pivoted to the middle seat, and shoved his hands under Noah's chin.

Matt's eyes widened as he watched the vomit—a partially digested replay of breakfast—fill his cupped hands and trickle through his fingers onto Noah's pants.

"What?" I sputtered. "Why?"

"I don't know…" he said, stunned. "I just reacted."

"I've never actually seen anyone projectile vomit before."

"Nooooooo. Me neither," Matt agreed, still shocked and surprised about what both he and our son had done.

Okay. Everything was going to be fine. Airplanes offer barf bags for this very reason. I grabbed one from the seat pocket in front of me. Now what? Should Matt pour the warm and chunky sludge into the bag? Open his hands and let it pour out the middle? I held the bag open as Matt tried to slide in his hands and their sour, chunk-filled contents.

"You go to the bathroom. I'll stay here and clean up Noah," I directed.

"I need you to take off my seat belt," he said, motioning with his unusable hands.

Leaning over our sick boy, I unhooked the belt and Matt shimmied out of his seat. Before he could head to the back of the plane, a flight attendant appeared.

"Excuse me, sir. Please stay in your…." The smell hit her before she realized what she was seeing. Recoiling, she grimaced and said, "Why don't you head to the restroom."

After Matt and his chaperone disappeared, I was left to handle the stinky, sticky, scared toddler.

"It's okay, you're okay, sweet boy," I whispered, smoothing his hair and drawing him close to me. He hiccupped and whined as I pulled off his dirty pants. Things weren't going well, but at least I had the foresight to pack a change of clothes for him. I knew planning would come in handy.

I put Noah onto my lap and kissed his head.

"Do you feel better now? Do you want some water or something to eat? It'll help get the taste out of your mouth." Once again, I was sure food was the answer.

He shook his head sadly. "It still hurts." He grimaced, then let out a stream of farts and giggled. At least he still had his sense of humor. No matter how sick you are, farts are always funny.

"Do you need to make a poop?" He farted again, this time so loudly I could feel it. Wait, that's not possible, is it? But I could feel it—it was a warm patch creeping over my leg. Oh no. Did I even want to look down? *No. No. No no no no no no no.* I did not, but I knew I had to. Taking a deep breath, I surveyed the damage.

Diarrhea was leaking out the leg hole of Noah's diaper. I gagged. Oh, shit. Literally. OH, SHIT. What was I going to do? Would picking him up make things worse? How long could I keep a kid on my lap who was wearing a leaking bag of shit?

As an experienced mom, I had dealt with my fair share of bodily fluids before. In fact, I'd worn all of them at some point. But this was different—I was trapped on a plane with a kid who was exploding from both ends. And while I had brought extra clothes for Noah, I hadn't brought anything extra for myself. I had not prepared for this. *Should I have worn my "lucky" socks? Did I not worry enough? Why didn't I know this was going to happen?*

I sighed with relief when Matt returned. "I think I won," I said as he looked down at us from the aisle.

"Huh?"

I pointed to my lap. And the small trickle of poop that was creeping farther and farther away from its source.

"Oh, wow. Wow."

"Yeah," I replied. "What do we do now?"

"Noah, can I take you to the bathroom to clean you off?"

Noah nodded. At least he felt better and wasn't complaining anymore.

"You can't walk down the aisle with him—he has poop dripping out of his diaper!"

"We can't get clean him here!"

"We'll just do the best we can and then you can take him to the bathroom to get the rest. See? I knew bringing the changing pad would come in handy."

Matt rolled his eyes.

We did the initial clean and then Matt made his way to the bathroom for the real cleaning job. Now that I was out of "fix it" mode, I needed to attend to the task at hand. A burp cloth wasn't going to be nearly enough to clean my befouled jeans but I had to try. I poured some of the water from Noah's bottle onto the cloth and began wiping my pants. *Eeeeeeeewwwwwwww.* I did as much as I could before I realized I had an escape hatch.

Xanax time. I grabbed my purse to find the only thing that could make this situation better. As I opened the pill box, the flight attendant materialized by our row.

"Ma'am?" the flight attendant asked kindly. "Can I help you with anything?"

"Oh, ha! Not unless you have any extra pants," I replied, trying to make light of the situation. I did a half smile and half shrug, just big enough to tilt the pill bottle, sending my one and only Xanax tumbling into the abyss between the armrest and the unreachable bottom of the seat.

*NO!!!!! No no no no no no no. First the indignity of being shit on and now my answer to it lost to the bowels of the plane?*

"Oh no!" The flight attendant said as she watched the pill tumble out. "I hope that wasn't important."

"Just a Tylenol," I said, trying to play it off as she left for better smelling parts of the plane.

I tried to look on the bright side. At least I didn't have to take off my pants, like I had to take off Noah's. They were gross but still wearable. But this is why moms tell you to wear clean underwear, right? In case you have to take off your shit-coated jeans, you're not showing off your torn, stained secrets to the world.

When Matt and Noah finally returned from the bathroom, it was time for my shit-covered walk of shame.

We spent the remainder of the flight trying our best to make Noah comfortable and to distract ourselves. He felt so lousy that he didn't want to do anything but sleep, rendering the rest of my overzealous packing job unnecessary.

When it was finally, FINALLY, time to deplane, I channeled my '90s teenaged self and tied my hoodie around my waist, carefully arranging the limp, noodle-like sleeve in front of the wet spot. Was the grossness camouflaged enough? Would the smell betray me? Was I engulfed in a cloud of stink like Pig-Pen?

I didn't really have a choice. The three of us shuffled off the plane, dazed and ready for Silkwood showers.

"Oh no," I said as my mom approached me for a hug at baggage claim, "you do *not* want to hug me."

"Do I even want to ask?"

"Poop. Your grandson pooped on me."

"You know what they say," my dad joked.

"Shit happens?" I said with a wry smile.

He smiled back.

"People make plans and God laughs," my mom chimed in.

"Yup. I understand that now."

That day I learned I can't control everything. Unexpected things are a part of parenting and part of life. They're often difficult to handle, gross, or smelly—in other words, they're shitty—sometimes literally. But if you're calm and have a good partner, it's possible to get through even the shittiest of parenting struggles. Plus, it's a good idea to carry extra clothes for everyone when you fly. Oh, and always carry more than one Xanax.

*This is JEN SIMON's sixth anthology, her second with Jen Mann. Although she writes about serious subjects like parenthood, depression, and addiction, she's also funny—TODAY* Parents, The Huffington Post, Babble, *and* Romper *all include her work often in funniest roundups. Jen has contributed to over two dozen websites including* The Washington Post, Cosmopolitan, Yahoo!, Redbook, Babble, Scary Mommy, *and many more.*

*You can follow Jen on Facebook, Twitter, and Instagram. Please see her website for more information:* www.jensimonwriter.com

# When the Birds and the Bees Are Dropping Like Flies
## By Michelle Poston Combs
### *Rubber Shoes in Hell*

"I think you need to just get it over with."

In retrospect, perhaps these words weren't the healthiest, affirming, or most reasonable advice to give my stepdaughter regarding her nonexistent sex life.

Hear me out, though. There were circumstances.

Kimberly was twenty-three years old at the time. We were having a few cocktails on the front porch with her grandmother, my mother-in-law. Perhaps those circumstances don't sound compelling enough to justify advocating my stepdaughter have casual sex, but a card laid is a card played. And she really did need to get laid.

Kimberly has been in my life since she was nine years old and while I didn't give birth to her, she's still my kid.

Kimberly has always been a "doing things on her own schedule" kind of person. She finished college with her lady garden unexplored and was feeling some stress about the situation.

Which brings us to the evening where my mother-in-law, Bonnie, and I entered opposite ends of a debate about my adult stepdaughter's virginity.

Kimberly consumed a few drinks after coming home from work. I'm thinking she probably should have eaten a sandwich. Even a peanut butter and jelly or some toast or something. But she didn't. She consumed tequila and told a sad, rambling tale of being a virgin and how she was never going to have sex. She told this tale to her grandmother.

Fortunately, her grandmother was nothing like either of my grandmothers. I would have chosen to fake a heart attack or perhaps gnaw off my own leg before discussing sex with either of my grandmothers.

Bonnie was a cool grandma, but she gave decidedly grandma-like advice. Bonnie patted Kimberly's knee. "Sweetheart, just stop worrying about it. It will happen and when it does, it will be magical."

"Hahahahahah." Laughing at my mother-in-law was not something I did often, but damn, she wasn't making any sense at all.

Bonnie raised an eyebrow. "What's so funny?"

I moved across the porch and settled in on the bench next to my stepdaughter. "Don't listen to her, Kimberly. The first time will not be magical. It will be sticky, probably mortifying, and very unlikely that you will get much from it, other than getting the first time over with. There will also be apologies. Pretty sure every first time comes equipped with a standard set of five apologies. Most of them will revolve around accidentally pulling your hair."

Bonnie flapped her hands in my direction. "Oh, no, sweetheart. That's not what will happen. You'll find yourself swept up in the moment and when it's over, you'll understand more about the woman you are becoming. It's a beautiful thing."

I sighed and drank the rest of my drink. "Okay, I guess we all have our definitions of beauty. But I've always thought an erect penis is kind of ridiculous looking."

Kimberly looked a bit like she might vomit. "I am not drunk enough for this."

I put my empty glass on the table in front of us and tried to ignore my mother-in-law's glare.

"Just find a nice boy you trust and seduce him. Make sure you bring protection. Get this one over with so that you don't have to feel weird about it anymore. Then, when you are in a relationship that gets sexual, you both won't be distracted by the whole 'losing your virginity' milestone."

Bonnie shook her head slowly. "Is that what you did to my son?"

"I'm your son's second wife."

Bonnie shrugged. "Good point. But you shouldn't make it sound so unappealing."

I put my head on Kimberly's shoulder. "The first time is unappealing."

Kimberly turned toward me. "How old were you when you had sex the first time?"

"We aren't talking about me right now, are we? I'm just saying, it is going to take you at least fifty go-arounds before you start, errr, hitting your stride. It takes a while to figure that shit out. It might even be 100 times. Plus, don't assume any partner is going to get it right. Speak up. Don't do things that hurt."

Bonnie sighed and opened the front door. "I need another daiquiri."

I'm not sure how much time passed between our chat on the porch that summer before Kimberly did the deed. I was glad when she finally got her first time over with and I was happy to help her jump that hurdle. After the hurdle was cleared, I didn't necessarily want to know anything specific about the actual jumping.

Kimberly had other plans and would take any opportunity to tell me about her sex life.

"Hey, Shell, you were right. It takes a while. I learned something around time thirty-six that really does it for me. Let me tell you about it."

I covered my ears with my hands. "No."

"Come on, it's really fun. It involves ice cubes, a rubber mask, and pin cushions."

I tried to play it cool. I did. But there was no way I was keeping the look of horror from my face. "No. And stay out of my sewing box."

Kimberly smiled. "That's what I call it now."

"Call what now?"

Her smile grew bigger. "My sewing box."

"I have created a monster."

I could complain about her torturing me with tales of her sexual prowess, but her bedroom was directly below the bedroom I shared with her father. We lived in an old house with high ceilings. Sound coming from other rooms sounded like they were coming from an echo chamber. I kind of owed her.

A few years after I gave her the sketchy advice, Kimberly had a daughter. I was lucky enough to watch the kid pop out. Kimberly and I had a few precious moments alone after she delivered her daughter, which she used to bitch at me. I completely lied to her when she was pregnant and scared of the pain of delivery. I told her that stubbing her toe was worse. She bought it.

Kimberly frowned at me. I knew that frown. That frown told me I'd pissed her off. "That hurt a lot more than stubbing my toe," she said.

I helped myself to some of her ice chips. "Yeah, I know. But you weren't worried as much, were you?"

She picked her plastic cup up and I dumped the rest of the ice in her cup. "Still," she said.

I sat on the bed next to her. "Okay. I am sorry I lied to you. I just didn't want you to be scared."

Kimberly adjusted her sheets and pulled herself up a little. "It's okay." She smiled the way she does when she's about to be a little shit. "Hey, Shell, you want me to tell you about the night she was conceived? Because there were props."

"No."

"I might even have a video."

I tapped her on the knee. "That advice is yours now to pass along. The torch is yours. We don't have to talk about it. Like ever again."

Kimberly rolled her eyes in a perfect imitation of her grandmother. "I don't think I'll be telling my daughter to just get sex over with."

I shrugged. "I was right though, wasn't I?"

I know it pains Kimberly to agree with me, but in this case, what else was she going to do?

"Oh, yes. Totally right," she said.

In retrospect, I could have done a better job with the "go have sex" talk, but I had no reference points. My sex talk with my mother consisted of talking about anything but sex.

I'd like to think I've learned my lesson. I just hope none of my granddaughters comes to me for sex advice. Unless we're having cocktails. Then I will tell her tales of how magical her first time will be.


*MICHELLE POSTON COMBS blogs at* Rubber Shoes In Hell. *She has contributed to* The Huffington Post, Better After Fifty, Midlife Boulevard,

Good Housekeeping, New Jersey Family Magazine, The Mid, MockMoms, Scary Mommy, Erma Bombeck Writers' Workshop, *and was in the 2015 Indianapolis cast of* Listen To Your Mother.

# Earn Your Keep
## Amy Flory
### *Funny Is Family*

I realized having kids would have its benefits the day my two-year-old son brought me a beer. The can was shaken beyond repair, but it was cold and I didn't have to get up to retrieve it myself, so I considered it a win.

Up until that magical moment, my kids had been takers. They took my body and then my sleep. They took my time and my milk. God's no dummy, so children are adorable and reek of feel-good pheromones, otherwise, no one would want them. They're greedy and useless.

Until they're not.

Now, this moment of usefulness comes at different times for different parents. Many moms would never have their toddler fetch them a beer, but if they did, they may not recognize the moment as a game-changer the way I did. I was drunk with the idea of other things I could make my boy do, and once his newborn sister could hold up her own head, she'd be in line for some chores too.

Admittedly, I'm lazy as all get out, but teaching my kids to help around the house has a bigger purpose than lightening my load. My job as a parent is to raise competent adults, which is no small feat. We're in a marathon, not a sprint, and raising human cubs takes time and effort.

When it came time for children to help around the house, we started small. My toddlers picked up toys and put them away, they stacked books in piles, and they put shoes in the shoe bin.

As preschoolers, my kids cut bananas with a butter knife and graduated to putting the books on bookshelves. They got themselves dressed and put dirty clothes in the hamper. They wiped up the gallons of bathwater that seemed to have no choice but to splash its way out of the tub.

By the time my son was in kindergarten, he was making his own sandwiches for lunch. He could vacuum the rug and put away his own clothing. He didn't do these things well, obviously. Both he and his sister have shirt and pants drawers that look like someone told them candy was buried at the bottom, but I turn a blind eye because the clothes are at least clean and put away.

Now, at seven and nine years old, my kids take out the garbage and unload the dishwasher. They can do their own laundry and fold their own clothes. They can strip their own bed and remake it with clean sheets.

My kids can make scrambled eggs and heat up canned soup. They can make sandwiches, toast, and oatmeal. They can cook pasta as long as an adult drains it because I'm not interested in tending to severe burns. They cut apples and cucumbers and peel hard-boiled eggs. Sure, I find bits of eggshell all over my kitchen, but when I hear "Mooooom, I'm hungry!" I don't always have to get up since they can whip up their own snacks.

This isn't to say my kids do all the household things they know how to do. They are much like both of their parents in that regard. They have school and Scouts and sports, and they need time to play with Legos and fight over stupid things, so I don't make them slop the metaphorical pigs as soon as they come home from school. But they know how to do things, because pitching in around the house is everyone's responsibility, and I want them both to marry well so they'll give me cute grandkids and take me on trips.

If you like the idea of tending to your child's every whim until they reach adulthood, and then probably even after that, this advice isn't for you. If you were thirsty just hearing about the two-year-old beer delivery system I mentioned in the first sentence, read on.

The key to encouraging kids to learn these important life skills is to lower your expectations. Imagine how you would like to see a task completed. Do you have it pictured? Now lower that bar. Lower. Actually, let's just put it on the ground for now. Kids do things terribly at first. They are so bad at stuff, it'll feel like they're screwing with you on purpose, like how I pretend I can't put air in my car tires because I would rather my husband do it for me.

Take cooking, for example. It's like learning to walk, only instead of a cute, chubby baby plopping to the ground, your kitchen is going to look like someone murdered the Pillsbury Doughboy because you let your preschooler measure the flour. Also, know that the sugar is now contaminated because your child's favorite booger finger is also the sugar-tasting finger. And be prepared for disappointment a few years later when your favorite egg pan is ruined because kids can't remember the important step of greasing a pan before scrambling eggs. I'll never forget my daughter's first solo attempt at oatmeal, mostly because the remnants will forever be cemented to the inside of the microwave.

When I was in high school, I mowed my grandparents' lawn. There were missed strips of long grass all over the yard, and my piss-poor job ensured that was the first and last time my papa had me do that job. I shouldn't have been surprised. Forty years earlier, as a newlywed, my grandmother mopped the kitchen floor. The end result didn't meet Papa's expectations, and he took over the floor mopping duties from then on out. My mother pulled a similar con job on my dad, and the tradition continues to this day. My kids may complete chores poorly, but I'm not falling for the oldest trick in the book, because I don't want to be cooking for them forever, and I really hate putting clothes away.

I wasn't terrible at all the tasks I was given as a child. I was great at doing dishes, I found immense satisfaction in vacuuming, and I could heat a can of tomato soup like no one's business. For an adult, these accomplishments seem ridiculous, but for a kid, they are solid resume builders. These household tasks filled me with pride for being such a good helper, but also with irritation because no matter how well you can load a dishwasher, it'll never be as much fun as reading a book. To this day, chores keep me from my books, although audiobooks have helped with this situation.

The thing is, I am a better human for all the cars I had to wash, coffee cups I had to refill, and trips to the basement I had to make for a gallon of milk or roll of paper towels. I swept patios and dusted shelves, I washed windows and scrubbed toilets, and I even mopped some floors, since my parents didn't have the same exacting standards as previously mentioned relatives. And I want this for my children too.

Kids can do chores earlier than many parents realize. Sure, they will do them badly for far too long, but eventually lowered expectations help your kids rise to the occasion. Just don't let them use the good frying pan.

*AMY FLORY has been featured on multiple parenting sites, was named one of* Mashable*'s 17 Funny Moms on Twitter, one of* Parenting*'s 10 Twitter Handles to Follow, and World's Meanest Mom by her kids. She is a contributor to the* New York Times *bestselling* I Just Want to Pee Alone *series, and the wildly popular* Big Book of Parenting Tweets *series. Amy is a big fan of eating, laughing, and her family, not necessarily in that order, and her blog,* FunnyIsFamily.com, *is a reflection of these passions.*

# Me, My Inferior Boobs, and My Green Baby
## By Elizabeth Hamilton Argyropoulos
### *Bourgeois Alien*

The hippest of hipster moms approached me in the park, gave me the once-over, and said in a tiny wisp of a voice yet still impossibly thick with judgment, "I ask that you not let your son offer his snacks to my child." She adjusted her handmade, locally sourced hemp scarf, which I can only assume was knitted by a local vegan shaman, adding, "We don't allow Atticus to eat that kind of food. Can I offer some advice?" Hipster Mom didn't pause for a response and this was obviously not a question. I desperately wanted to interrupt:

Look, sister, you're better than me. I get it. We all get it. Even your snacks are better. And okay sure, I'm also a bit of a hipster douche, but I have enough self-awareness to be a quiet, self-loathing hipster douche. Now please kindly piss off.

But I didn't say that or anything, probably because I'm a bit of a moron and also because I obviously love being abused by pretentious strangers on warm summer days. Sadly, I could see Hipster Mom had a monologue prepared for which I was lucky enough to be the sole audience member and she intended to perform posthaste. She looked stoically at the sky, paused for dramatic effect, and finally began, "In our house, we follow the golden rule: real snacks come in their own wrappers."

I don't mean to be boastful, but I had just witnessed the Merriam-Webster definition of smug. Please, don't be jealous. I can't help it if I'm lucky and you're not. But that was it, strangely succinct. I have to hand it to her; brevity truly is the source of wit. Only, it wasn't supposed to be funny. Sorry I laughed a little, Hipster Mom. She gave me a self-congratulatory half smile and went back to her son, now eating his boogers in the middle of the playground. Well, I thought, at least boogers come in natural wrappers—noses.

Me, in 2009, when it happened: I'm sorry; I didn't know my son was sharing his snacks. I'll make sure he keeps them to himself.

Me, if this happened now: Maybe Atticus should be put in a bubble to protect him from everything that doesn't meet your standards and in twenty years they'll make a movie about him called, *The Hipster Douche's Boy in the Plastic Bub*ble.

Yes, that was a 1976 *The Boy in the Plastic Bubble* joke. I keep my references fresh, like gas station sushi. Periodically when I'd fall asleep at night I'd often think about that moment and mumble witty comebacks, much to my husband's chagrin:

Maybe if you gave your kid a snack once in a while he wouldn't be standing in the middle of the playground eating his own boogers.

Surely your alien leaders explained the concept of sharing before they dropped you off here.

My son shared his snacks? Walk, nay, run to your nearest emergency room to check if little Atticus has an adverse reaction, or even worse, to see if he was infected with my family's mediocrity.

Maybe part of the problem is I've never been one of those seemingly natural mothers and can be too sensitive. And no, I don't mean natural as in smells and looks like a family of ferrets died under their arms. Look, I'm not being cruel saying this. I grew up in a hippie town and that is a perfectly accurate assessment of that entire unseemly situation under there. What I mean is it appears mothering comes naturally to some women, and by contrast I wind up feeling crushingly insecure. I have friends it seems were born to be moms. They were comfortable with the advice they presented themselves as an expert on and gave it out regularly, but I, however, was never sure.

My ambiguity stems from seeing all sides of any issue and reading everything I can get my hands on. And no, this isn't wishy-washy, I simply know I know nothing: Socrates, bitches. A modicum of self-doubt is an important thing in life. And let's be honest here, it's usually not the sharpest knives in the drawer constantly trying to shove their opinions down your throat with absolute certainty.

My personal nosedive into the relentless insecurity that is parenting began in Athens, Greece. From moment one of my pregnancy, my husband's family wanted to control everything. If you've ever spent time with Greeks, you know *reserved* isn't an adjective that immediately springs to mind. I wish modern Greeks would take the advice of the ancient Greeks and have a little uncertainty. It seems modern Greeks have updated Socrates's expression to read, "I know that I know everything. Don't question me. I have spoken." I had moved to the land of experts and perpetual advice. All of a sudden I wasn't me, but a baby oven, and every woman in Greece had the best recipe and none of them was in agreement. But really, who doesn't love being constantly bossed around?

Luckily, they spoke so quickly, and my Greek wasn't perfect, that I usually only got about half of what they said. Even though my husband offered to translate everything, I almost always declined. Their guidance became something like the Rorschach inkblots of advice—they'd talk and I'd hear whatever I wanted, always nodding my head in agreement. After a while, I'd look forward to the barrage of indecipherable advice, "Okay, I see. You said that I should ask my husband to take me to Paris before the baby comes and eat this entire cake today by myself? Also, I should make a hat out of bananas? That's a great idea, Dimitra, thank you." Of course, knowing my husband's exceedingly cheap family they probably said, "Don't waste money on the luxury of store-bought bread and milk. You should bake all day and buy a goat to milk, you spoiled American. Oh, and everything you do is wrong, in case you forgot. You're welcome."

Since I barely understood most of the advice thrown at me, I did what I felt was best and decided on a natural birth. Wanting everything to be natural, I even let a family of ferrets live under my arm. I was in a foreign land, why not? I'd smell like a Coachella porta-potty if I wanted to. And honestly, keeping people away has always been a life goal of mine; why not start now with my paint-peeling hippie stink?

The next several months, I came to my obstetrician's appointments with a notepad of questions. My doctor often said through a forced, halfhearted chuckle, "You Americans with all your questions—I just love it." No, she didn't. She sometimes rolled her eyes so hard while we were talking that I was convinced she was giving herself a rectal exam. Hey, doc, not on my dime, you don't. At one point she suggested I stop reading my pregnancy books so I wouldn't worry so much. However, when my water broke two weeks early I knew because of the green color my son was in distress. She finally said, "You helped save his life. Good thing you read and knew to get him in right away."

While recovering in the hospital after my C-section, the Greek nurses spoke about me like I wasn't there, assuming I didn't know Greek. And please trust me when I say I wished I didn't understand. By that point my Greek was improving and I knew enough to know they were calling my son πράσινο μωρό or in English, "the green baby." My son was the only blond kid and the meconium had tinted his hair green. Punk rock.

Ugh. The Green Baby. Well, I thought, trying to cheer myself up, look on the bright side: sure, you didn't get to have a natural birth, but at least "The Green Baby" sounds natural. This idiotic cheering up didn't work. In fact, it felt like I was taunting myself. I've always wished I had a bouncer to throw out the hecklers in the third-rate comedy club that is my head.

And on top of having green hair Alexander was the only one who cried constantly, so they lengthened his already stellar nickname to, "the green baby who always cries." Of course he's crying all the time. Didn't the nurses ever hear Kermit's song "It's Not Easy Being Green"? Didn't the Greeks have Kermit? The cherry on the souvlaki was when the nurses went on and on right in front of me about how foreign women have inferior boobs because Greek women are superior milk producers. I imagined them discussing each other at parties, "Oh you know Maria, sure you do, the superior milk producer," and all the other Greek women would say, "Ohhh…that Maria!" and nod in agreement about Maria's prodigious milk-gushing Greek ta-tas.

I spent the first three days of motherhood miserable….just me, my inferior boobs, and my green baby. You'd think that would have prepared me for the tough road ahead, but no. I always have to learn the hard way because as I explained to you before, I am a moron.

When I got home, my husband's relatives told me I should never pick up a crying baby because it would spoil him. I had already decided on attachment parenting and ignored them the best I could. That first year as a mother in Greece was a lot like being public property. Old women would run up to me in the Greek summer heat, cover my son's head, and yell at me for letting my son freeze to death in 100-degree weather. I got yelled at constantly by old women in Athens for a host of things I'm still not sure I understand. Probably for being too tall, I don't know. I decided I needed to go home and visit my mom before I beat a bossy Greek motherfucker with another bossy Greek motherfucker.

In America, I told my mom while crying like a big, ridiculous baby-lady that everyone was telling me I was doing everything wrong and I felt like a broken mess. My mom stroked my hair and gave me the best piece of parenting advice I ever received, "My darling, shut it all out—all of it. It's natural to have self-doubt. But you must listen to your instinct; do what you feel is right and all the rest will fall into place." Easy for her to say, I thought, she was done with the nightmare of raising her idiot daughter.

I went to sleep that night and had a dream my son, then eleven months, said "I love you" for the first time. The next morning he toddled down my parents' hall and said, "I wub you, Mama." It was a deeply moving almost religious experience, and frankly I'm not a religious person at all. In fact, I'm a fallen Catholic. How fallen? you ask. I actually fell in front of the Vatican. This is true and completely not my fault. The marble there has been walked on for so many hundreds of years it's as slippery as glass. Fix that mess. Fallen Catholics are totally on you, Vatican.

The important thing was I was happy for the first time in a long time. My darling green baby said I love you, and I took that as a sign it was time to start listening to my own instinct and anyone who tried to make me feel less than would now be categorized under the same file in my brain where I keep people who say, "awesomesauce" and "totes," forever written off as dead to me. From then on, I was empowered. Nobody would intimidate me, I was on my way, and I was going to be fierce. And I lived happily ever after secure in my very own maternal wisdom.

The End.

Of course, I'm just kidding. You'd have to find out where I lived and punch me in my inferior boobs if I ended it there. Oh dear God no, this is real life, not the end of a sitcom where everyone inexplicably freezes mid motion after learning some slack-jawed TV morality lesson. No, it's an ongoing battle with mothering insecurity. Yes, this advice my mom gave me was there. It was in my head, but so was self-doubt, and like any parent who cares, a voice that said, "What if I'm doing this all wrong? What if I ruin him? Even worse, what if Green Baby grows up and uses words like awesomesauce?"

By the time Alexander was four we moved back to the United States. My son had no problems adjusting to his new country. He would often walk up to strangers and proudly introduce himself, "Hi, I'm Alexander. Don't let the blond hair fool you, I'm Greek!"

My son had confidence in spades; me, not so much.

In many ways, parenthood has broken its foot off in my ass repeatedly the past twelve years, not because of my son, but in dealing with other parents. I sincerely wish parents would try harder to lift each other up rather than tear each other down. I never knew parenting was going to be a competitive sport until I became one. And anyone who knows me knows this simple truth: Beth is bad at sports and hasn't seen a football, basketball, or baseball game since high school. I'd rather be dragged face down in mud than sit through a sporting event. For this year's Super Bowl Sunday I binge-watched *Six Feet Under* again and ordered Thai food, if that gives you any indication of my sportiness. Also, the one time I tried to throw a Frisbee I broke my mom's bay window not understanding what trajectory is because yes, I am also a moron at math.

Yet somehow in spite of all the parenting insecurity I found the strength to frequently trust my instinct. I let my son pursue technology when my hipster friends told me to only let him play with wooden toys. At nine, Alexander built computers for my entire family and at eleven he taught a Google technology summer camp. I homeschool him and have made many choices that are far left of center. Almost a teen, I've even let Alexander occasionally swear at home if he feels that's what the situation requires. And at age twelve, my thoughtful green boy is the friend who often explains why it's cruel to body shame, reads political articles, and then can factually argue anyone into the ground on a host of important issues. Did you know studies show that people who swear occasionally tend to be smarter and more empathetic? These are facts. Look, if you're offended by bad words, don't be angry at me, be angry at science: stupid fucking science.

It's not often in life you get a redo, but once in a while a bit of luck is sent your way and you get to set a few things straight.

Hipster Mom: My son heard your son say "damn" at your house on their playdate. We don't allow our children to speak that way. We feel that it's wrong to swear for any reason—it's detrimental to their development.

Me: I see. Listen, while I have your ear, can you make sure Atticus stops picking on other children for their physical appearance? The other child at their playdate spent the day in tears. Oh, you didn't know that was the issue? Huh, weird. Well, in our house we follow the golden rule: we believe in intent and what words mean, not just so-called "bad" words. We believe hurting someone for a cheap laugh is detrimental to their development.

It turns out when you say exactly what you intend to say the moment you intend to say it, you have no problems sleeping. Isn't that marvelous? And my husband hasn't heard me mumbling insults in my sleep in months.

We now sleep like adorable green babies.


*ELIZABETH HAMILTON ARGYROPOULOS has always thought of herself as funny. Not "funny ha ha" but more of a "ha ha, wow…that's sad" kind of funny. A Miami native, she moved to study improv at Second City in Chicago. While living there and being very funny indeed, she met and moved to Greece for almost a decade with her equally funny Greek husband, Steve. They now live in Florida with their son, Alexander, who is funnier than both of them.*

*In addition to* But Did You Die?, *she is currently working on a series of hysterical essays for a book about her curious experiences as an American woman living in Greece.*

*Beth's tweets are consistently featured all over the web. She was on* Playboy's 50 *funniest tweeters of 2016,* The Huffington Post, Mandatory, Funny or Die, ELLE, Mashable, Berry, Thought Catalog, *and* Chicago Tribune *to name a few.*

*Follow her on her website elizabethargyropoulos.com, on Twitter, or on Facebook.*

# My Cooking Lessons Smelled Like Darwinism and Old Chicken Poop

By Kim Bongiorno

*Let Me Start By Saying*

I'll give my mom this: she maintained her relentless optimism during the approximately eighteen years of fruitlessly trying to teach me how to properly boil water while not burning the house down. She was a self-taught cook whose love language was making meals from scratch—and she desperately wanted me to be a part of that process.

Our home was the perfect stage for my lessons: my father deliberately bought a house with a backyard that once held a chicken coop—because decades of fowl feces made great garden fertilizer ("just like in the old country")—and my mom had every recipe book and gadget ever created tucked away in our little kitchen. They would raise children who were comfortable picking, prepping, and cooking their own food, whether we wanted to or not.

The closest I ever came to showing interest in living the farm-to-table life was popping a thick slug into my mouth while wandering through our tangle of tomato plants as a tot. Sure, I almost choked to death on it, but once my parents saw I was still alive, they were thrilled that I took the initiative to be in the garden at all!

And so it began.

I don't ever remember a time when I was not either collecting produce to cook or wielding an implement to cook it with. On steamy summer days when my friends were riding bikes to the corner store to buy Pop Rocks and Pepsi, I was tapping thigh-sized eggplants to check for ripeness, while ankle-deep in petrified ancient chicken poo. I spent hours in that garden watching sweet peppers bloom and delicate string beans dangle in the hot breeze, while swatting away flittering bugs investigating the speckled green bowl of zucchini under my arm and wondering how I'd ever find a boy who liked me when I was the weird girl who always smelled a little bit like the special plant food my mom made from eggshells and used coffee grounds.

Sure, it was nice my parents valued an important life skill they wanted to impart to their offspring, but it was often a lot more like being Beetle Bailey peeling his way through a mountain of potatoes under the watch of Sergeant Snorkel than Giada De Laurentiis sautéing garlic with a pearly white smile for a captive audience. On more than one occasion, a friend would pop over to our Cape during one of many tomato sauce jarring weekends to discover me in the midst of what looked like Dexter's kill room, only to run away when my mom invited them to join us because it was "so much more fun than it looked." (LIES.)

From toddlerhood to high school, my parents insisted it was important for me to learn how to properly make ravioli on the same creaky equipment my great-great-grandma did back in Italy, bake a cake from scratch that didn't collapse in the middle, or at least manage one solitary batch of Rice Krispies treats without burning them (nope, nope, and nope).

Over the years, they tried every recipe from sweets to savories, and nothing stuck. Unless, of course, you consider the plastic toy steak I managed to melt inside an unsuspecting oven in an early attempt at independent cooking. I repeatedly ruined flea market pans (they knew not to buy anything new or fancy) and wasted ingredients—but at least I tried. And tried and tried. My parents gave me absolute groundless trust in the kitchen with hot, sharp, and burnable things in the hope I would maybe not starve to death once I moved out of our home. But the truth of the matter is: all I left that house with was a bunch of scars on my forearms from yanking things out of the oven that I had managed to light on fire, the ability to heat up SpaghettiOs (the good kind with the sliced hot dogs) to a safe temperature, and a high tolerance for the scent of chicken dung.

It wasn't until I was in my late twenties that I finally got the hang of how to use an oven. Shortly thereafter, I ended up with a bun in my own. It was then that I decided my parents were onto something—and I simply had to impart my newfound cooking skills on my kids.

When my son was two and my daughter was nine months old, we moved into a house with a beautiful open-plan kitchen that begged to be used, and I started imagining the kind of mental reel that movie montages were made of: the three of us in matching aprons lit by shimmering golden afternoon sunlight, stirring the pungent ingredients of some mouthwatering concoction in various pots. I couldn't wait to begin making forever memories with them in there.

That was until my daughter began an interesting eighteen-month phase during which she was obsessed with climbing into the hot oven. Yes, you read that correctly: the *hot* oven. The cold oven did not interest her at all; it was only when that beast was cranked up to 450ºF, she was all, "Get me in your belleh!" She could be playing anywhere in the house, but when the gentle click of the oven turning on sounded, she'd appear like Pavlov's masochistic dog to try to roast herself in her own personal incinerator. Because of that, I had to learn to cook with one hand while having the other ready for defensive tactics. Hooray for forced ambidextrousness!

When this all started, I had been hosting weekly play-date dinners at my home. Now, when the moms and their kids came over each week, I was forced to assign one mother to sit by the oven to keep my kid out of it while I dashed back and forth prepping our meals. Not exactly convenient to making us seem like a normal family.

It went something like this: "Hi. Come on in. Oh, and can you please make sure my daughter doesn't crawl into the oven with the lasagna? I have to go make sure my son didn't take his pants off again."

By the time my youngest finally stopped her kitchen death runs, I was so used to shouting, "GET OUT OF THE KITCHEN" that my desire to teach them to cook or do any food prep at all had completely disappeared. From dicing their grapes into dust-particle-sized bites when they were toddlers to toasting and buttering their bagels when they were in elementary school, I had taken it all over to ensure my children's safety. So ingrained was this reflex that I never even *thought* to have my kids help me in the kitchen at all anymore. I had created a No Kid Zone in the ten-foot radius around the microwave and oven, and practically *Karate Kid* crane-kicked my crew outta there should they so much as toe the invisible line.

That's why when I walked in on my seven-year-old daughter wielding a knife the approximate length of her right arm, I did what most traumatized parents would do: I freaked the freak out. Dogs, and dogs alone, could hear the decibel level of my panicked squeal.

I crept up on that girl like a ninja at midnight and swooped the blade from her little grip. After shunting her to the next room and breathing into a slightly used brown lunch bag while imagining all the ways she could have sliced and diced her little phalanges into bite-sized pieces, I calmed down and looked at the kitchen counter. There was a kaleidoscope of washed vegetables laid out with buttery croutons, a selection of dressings, Italian seasoning, and a big mixing bowl. The garbage trimmings were set aside (à la Rachael Ray—seriously, was the kid secretly watching chef shows behind my back?), and there were place settings for four, neatly stacked on the end closest to the kitchen table. My daughter had been making a chopped salad for the family, and had plans to serve it to us for dinner.

She did it all without help, and she was perfectly fine.

Maybe it was time for me to let go of my fears and let my kids back in the kitchen?

I managed to survive an entire childhood during which I was expected to at least try all the same cooking my parents did, because being independent in the kitchen was a valued trait in our family. That constant brush with Darwinism carried over to the rest of my life, too, and I proved to be the kind of person who was willing to take careful risks while working the recipe until I got it right—or at least right enough for me. My parents weren't particularly concerned with exactly how I was getting by in the kitchen (knives and whatnot); they just wanted me in the kitchen, learning as I went along. And so that's what I did.

Their strategy worked to my benefit in the end. I survived my experience and ended up becoming not only an independent woman, but a damn fine cook, as well. So, why was I getting in the way of my daughter experiencing that too?

With that question looming in mind, I invited her back into the kitchen, wiped her tears and walked her through the proper way to hold the knife—a *much smaller* knife. I stepped back to let her finish the meal, a nervous spectator hoping this show ended well. And it did: it was delicious!

From there, we moved on to how to use the toaster, the blender, a number of other gadgets, and, eventually, her former frenemy: the oven.

I gave her the same trust and knowledge that was given to me in my childhood when I'd nearly burned down my own mom's kitchen while trying to find my place in it, and am happy to report it has been going very well. I don't think I'll ever regret finally letting *her* be the one to figure out when she was getting too close to the flame (while making sure she knew exactly where the fire extinguisher and first-aid kit were, of course). She's been flourishing in the kitchen ever since, and I've been enjoying the victorious fruits of her labor.

Every last sweet bite of them.

*KIM BONGIORNO is the* author and freelance writer *behind the blog* Let Me Start By Saying. *A crafter of everything from funny parenting tweets to fantastical fiction, her work has received praise from the likes of Buzzfeed,* The Huffington Post, *the* TODAY Show, *and the* Erma Bombeck Writers' Workshop. *Kim lives in New Jersey with her family, who she pretends to listen to while playing on* Facebook *and* Twitter. *If she were less tired, she'd totally add something really clever to her bio so you'd never forget this moment. Find her on Facebook and Twitter. Learn more at* KimBongiornoWrites.com.

# Parenting Advice from the Childless Voice of Reason
## By Aussa Lorens
### *Hacker.Ninja.Hooker.Spy.*

The problem with most parenting advice is that it comes from parents. You can't trust those people. It's already too late for them and they want to make sure they're not the only ones who ruin their children. Misery loves company and no one is more miserable than a parent who's bought into the idea that an "expert" is going to help them.

As a childless thirty-year-old woman I feel I'm the only person qualified to speak to this situation. I've watched too many of my college friends fall victim to the blight of "sleep training" and "positive reinforcement," and can no longer stay silent. I've seen you bartering with your toddler in the checkout line at Target because they can't live without a $4 piece of garbage that'll probably never make it out of your minivan. I've watched you at restaurants, begging your kid to eat the mac-n-cheese they wanted until it was in front of them and they realized they hate that shade of yellow.

Let me help. You don't need to add anything else to your to-do list, you just need to cease and desist with the following:

*Obsessing over developmental milestones*
The only thing "educational" about wooden toys and faux laptops is the marketing strategy behind them. Your kid will be too clever for their own good, with or without your interference. Before you know it they'll ask questions you can't answer and burn you with comebacks worthy of an HBO special. Why rush it?

I know you want your kid to grow up and be super smart and zero fun at parties, but they're probably just going to laugh at farts like the rest of us. If you insist upon trying to teach your baby, I suggest you start with the following difficult-to-pronounce words:

First Word: Sit

Second Word: Fork

Imagine all the ways they can use this in a sentence, like "I have no forks left to give" and "I'm going to sit on you."

Stop saying stuff like this: "We're practicing how to grasp items so she can reach her next developmental stage."

Do you really think your baby won't figure out how to pick up every single thing you don't want it to touch? Take them to a public park. Dog poo, cigarette butts, and used needles are all the incentive your baby needs to learn "how to grasp." Can I make a suggestion? Try and stunt their development. Show me a baby that can't grab a dangling earring and I'll show you a contender for Parent of the Year.

*Letting Nature be your pediatrician*

I enjoy burning sage and sending my intentions to the universe as much as the next person, but when your kid is sick you should probably take it to a doctor. This is not the time to excitedly break out the fanny pack of essential oils your high school bestie pressured you into buying after you accepted her friend request.

Lavender oil: Does smell amazing

Lavender oil: Does not treat bacterial infections

I know you spent several hundred dollars on .02 ounces of nothing, but you need to do what the rest of us do and stash it in the back of your bathroom cabinet where you never have to see it again.

Stop saying stuff like this: "People have been using this health remedy for thousands of years."

This might be true but those people didn't have indoor plumbing or a life expectancy beyond thirty-five. Make up your mind—do you want to have dirt floors and never travel farther than five miles from your house? Probably not. Welcome to the future and welcome to not dying because you stubbed your toe on a piece of metal.

I know it's super vintage and #Throwback but please vaccinate your offspring. Don't force the rest of us to live an alternate plotline from *The Mummy* where a small number of stupid people resuscitate an apocalyptic scourge we already dealt with forever ago.

I'm not telling you what to believe, but there's a pretty good chance someone with a PhD in immunology knows more than Judy in Dayton, Ohio, who bought the domain NaturalHealthLifeStuff.Net.

I know you're waiting for more conclusive research but SPOILER WARNING: Smallpox kills people and the bubonic plague is the sequel no one wants to see.

*Trying to convince the Internet your life is perfect*

It's possible no one told you this, but most babies don't trot out of the birth canal dressed for a night at the theater. Yes, you can buy Burberry galoshes in size 0 and order a $400 child-size teepee they'll never play with, but this stuff only makes sense when posed for a photograph.

What your search history tells us: "Kid swallowed a pool float is that bad?"

What your social media tells us: "Perfect weather for a pool day!"

Don't try to lie to the Internet. It knows all your secrets anyways.

Stop saying stuff like this: "I'm preserving our memories!"

Someday your kid is going to look at your old photos and wonder why they don't remember playing near an artistically abandoned warehouse (complete with the perfect juxtaposition of peeling paint and wildflowers). Do you really want to tell them it's because they repressed the memory of you yelling "Mommy needs this for her Insta!" while they held back tears and got in trouble for asking why all those people have shopping carts and are warming their hands over a burning trash can?

Capturing your child standing perfectly still while staring wistfully at an eagle feather or partially blown dandelion isn't exactly an accurate image of childhood. Unless of course you're dosing them with Benadryl first.

*Acting like your kid is qualified to make decisions about anything other than when to poop*

Your kid's brain is still developing; it isn't in a position to make important decisions. Would you invest in a company whose mission statement is: "Eat, Cry, Poop, Cry"? Then stop letting them choose what you're having for dinner. THEY'RE NOT GOING TO EAT IT ANYWAY.

Your kid says: "But why?"

You say: "Because I can make another one that looks just like you."

You don't owe your toddler an explanation. Their vocabulary is smaller than a golden retriever's; they probably can't even understand you.

Stop saying stuff like this: "Sweetie, that bowl has porous wood and the oil from your fingers will damage the integrity of the surface."

Unless your kid is paying for it, they should have zero say in where your family goes for vacation. Save yourself thousands of dollars by taking them to the loading zone behind Home Depot. All those stacked boxes and pieces of broken equipment will result in the same combination of wonder and emotional meltdown as a trip to Disney World.

Honestly, they're not even going to remember where you took them. But the rest of us will. Because you ruined our vacation.

*Making excuses for your toddler's behavior*
The only time you need to explain your toddler's behavior is when they act uncharacteristically calm and reasonable. If they're throwing things, screaming, and acting like a megalomaniac sociopath then rest assured your child is behaving in accordance with nature. They're not "going through a phase." They're realizing what the rest of us already know—that most of life is putting on pants and doing as you're told—and they still have the wherewithal to protest.

Current phase: terrible

Next phase: terrible

Don't even ask if it gets better. There's a light at the end of the tunnel but it's on the other side of braces, driver's ed, and college tuition.

Stop saying stuff like this: "I'm so sorry, he's not usually like this. He must be tired/hungry/going through an Oedipal phase where I must ignore my husband and devote myself exclusively to my offspring."

Remember all those times you helped your drunk friend home from the bar after $3 Wine Wednesday? It's time to put those skills back to use. Your growing bundle of joy is basically a miniature sorority girl who can't figure out how to use her Uber app and just wants someone to give her French fries and tell her she's pretty.

*Viewing your kid as a do-over for your own disappointing childhood*
Remember how your parents are to blame for all your problems? Your kids will feel the same way. It's the circle of life and the harder you try to not repeat your parents' failure, the weirder things are going to get. Your parents didn't love you enough? You'll shower your kid with affection. Your parents coddled you too much? You'll probably be too hard on your kids.

Your Generation: complains about the next generation

Next Generation: complains about your generation

Welcome to the self-sustaining cycle of everyone ruining everything in an attempt to not ruin things.

Stop saying stuff like this: "I just want to give her everything I never had."

I know this is hard for you to hear right now, but no one needs sixteen American Girl dolls. I promise your child will still become a reasonably productive member of society whether or not you give her every single thing you believe you missed out on.

*Listening to so much advice*
If all of this feels overwhelming, just remember: No one else knows what they're doing either. You'll be fine.

*AUSSA LORENS is the writer behind* Hacker.Ninja.Hooker.Spy. *where some mistakes are too good not to share. Despite dropping out of college to backpack around the world, working at a psych ward (where the staff were crazier than the patients), and making a score of terrible relationship choices, she now lives in Denver with her husband and their Rhodesian ridgeback. She promises not to compare her dog to your child. At least not while you're in the room.*

*Her work has been published on* Narrative.ly, Cosmopolitan, Marie Claire, Elle, *and* The Huffington Post. *You can find her online at* aussalorens.com *or visit her on Twitter* @AussaLorens.

# Always Change the Batteries
## By Victoria Fedden


I'm pretty useless when it comes to parenting advice. Sure, I've managed to keep a small human being alive for six-plus years now, but that, by no means, makes me any kind of reliable expert, especially when it comes to raising little ones. Breast or bottle? I don't know. Feed them. As long as it's not spicy Bloody Mary mix in the sippy cup you're probably okay. Diapers? No. Freaking. Clue. As soon as my kid was potty trained (which she did on her own so don't ask me about that either) I promptly forgot how diapers even worked, much like the way you forgot everything about the Civil War except emancipation immediately after you took your American History midterm. I have repressed all memories of infant and toddler care, so when new parents come to me for help, all I've got for them is this:

Keep a lot of batteries on hand.

You're going to need more batteries than you ever thought possible, and make sure you change the batteries in your child's toys often. I learned this lesson the hard way, of course, because that's how I prefer to do things, apparently.

The whole battery thing didn't so much as sneak up on me as sucker-punch me in the back of the head, and it happened on a dark and stormy night, but before we get to that part, let me give you a little background here.

When I was pregnant I had full-fledged delusions that my baby was going to play with all-natural, dye-free, 100 percent wood and hemp and organic cotton toys, which I imagined to be handmade by sweet-tempered Scandinavian elves. We would have no garish plastic, no gaudy primary colored, racket-making brain rotters stifling imaginations in our pleasant (and spotlessly uncluttered) home! I would fashion small woodland animals from felted wool for my daughter to play with, and I would likely do so in my thriving biodynamic garden while I nibbled on free-range placenta chips. Or something. I believed this because:

1. I didn't know myself very well, and
2. I had no idea what was about to happen and how I would be entirely powerless to stop it.

When a couple has a child, the new parents are often blessed by the generosity of many well-meaning friends and relatives, and other people who are absolutely desperate to get rid of their older children's gratingly irritating, jingle-tinkling, trash-talking junk toys. You get a lot of new toys as gifts and you get a lot of hand-me-down toys too, and obviously if you tried to refuse any of it, you'd come off looking like an ungracious jerk-face, so you smile and say thanks and then the crap starts piling up. All of it is going to be plastic, and primary colored. All these toys will need batteries. There will be a lot of noise. By the time my kid celebrated her first birthday, I was ready to run screaming from my home to hide in one of those ashrams where people take vows of silence to meditate for weeks on end, because there was just so much noise coming from electronic toys, none of which I'd purchased or had been crafted by gentle gnomes. You should also know I didn't have that garden and the closest we got to felted animals was when my daughter crawled under the bed and dragged out some dust bunnies.

As a toddler, my daughter's favorite toy was a remote-controlled cat that rolled along our tile floors seemingly of its own volition, while digitally meowing in a plaintive, electronic mew. I swear to you, this thing would purposely chase me around the house. It had eyes that lit up and flashed, and my child adored this horrible plastic cat, but I felt it had real malicious intent. I didn't trust the cat. I didn't trust any of it, but we kept it because naturally, the baby really liked these toys! They maintained her attention. The hemp dolls and wooden—well, yeah, I couldn't afford them, so there weren't any.

And then, right around her first birthday, my mother thought it would be funny to buy her granddaughter her first car. It was harmless, right? No. No, it wasn't. Little did I know, the car was demon possessed. It was the toddler version of *Christine,* except at first, the car seemed ordinary, because that's what always happens in *Twilight Zone* episodes. It was one of those little cars that toddlers can sit on and scoot themselves across the floor with their feet, Fred Flintstone style. It was pink and lavender and pale yellow. It was decorated with Disney princess stickers, and there were several buttons and doo-hingers all over it that would make noise when messed with. Excessive noise. Incredibly annoying noise. It sang songs much like the ice cream truck. It had honking horns and chimes and bells that went ding and knobs you could flip and handles you could pull *and they all made noise*. My mother had found the car at Ross and claims she "fell in love with it," but I'm convinced she bought it as some form of calculated revenge for all the noise I made to irritate her when I was a child. I had a green plastic recorder and a real harmonica, you see.

The car was so cacophonous that I put it outside and declared it an "Outside Toy" much to my toddler's dismay, but I'm sorry, Mommy's misophonia comes first! You may ask why I didn't simply turn it off. Here's the catch. It had no on/off switch I could ever locate. That doesn't necessarily mean there wasn't one. It just meant I never found it if it existed. I'm not exactly the most technologically savvy person around, if you hadn't already figured that out.

For several months, I managed to at least moderately tolerate the electronic toys that had invaded my home, and I never bought batteries. Nor did I consider that these toys would ever run low on power. I blame exhaustion. By that time we had not just the cat and the car, but also some singing microphones, a doll that told us when she had to pee, which was so often that I was about to get her checked for diabetes, and a large pink-and-purple castle that not only played an entire symphony if you even glanced at it, but also came with seven princesses who each sang ballads from their hit films. Yes, I said SEVEN of them. Then there was the realistically whinnying unicorn that clearly had a lot of grievances to air because it never shut up, and so many crying baby dolls that my daughter's room sounded like the Duggars' house.

But soon my temporary truce with the racket would fall to pieces.

Like I said it was a dark and stormy night. No really. It was. It was about midnight and my husband and I were in bed and the wind was howling outside. When the gales hit our fence and whip through the spaces between the boards, the noise is bone chilling. No banshee could ever compete. But through all that, something else managed to keep me awake: Music. Music was playing. It wasn't rock or pop or even EDM. This was something far more sinister, a bit like the soundtrack to every Tim Burton film ever made.

Here is where I'd get killed in a horror movie: I went to investigate the mysterious noise. At first I thought my husband had left the TV on, so I went to check. Nope. TV off. I looked everywhere. Was it a phone? No. Something in the baby's room? No. Finally, I realized the music was coming from outside. Maybe my husband left the porch stereo on by accident. I went into the porch. Stereo off.

But once I was outside, I could hear the music more clearly and then it hit me. The car. The toy car was going through its entire repertoire of songs and ding-a-lings—its overture of madness.

Not caring that I was barefoot and wore nothing but an old T-shirt and my husband's boxers, I stalked out into the backyard in the wind and rain with a mission. I would silence the toy car so all could sleep in peace. I yanked it up by its handle and shook the damned thing, but it played its creepy carousel song seemingly louder, as if it knew, and carousel music is way eerier when played outside at night *in a storm*.

Illuminated only by flashes of lightning, I flipped the toy car over looking for an on/off switch. Nothing. Maybe if I took it inside, I thought, out of the rain and darkness, I could give it a good look-over and find some way to cut its power.

Once inside, on my dining room floor, to be exact, I switched the lights on and tried to find a way to turn the car off, but it played on persistently, getting louder and louder. I began to feel desperate and I nearly had a heart attack when the electronic cat buzzed past me, eyes flashing.

"MEW! MEW!" it snarled.

By this point, the racket had awakened my husband, who found me huddled over a wet toy car, dripping and frantic on the dining room floor.

"I can't make it stop!" I cried.

"Just take the battery out," he mumbled, shuffling back to our room and firmly closing the door behind him.

Why hadn't I thought of that?

But great. The battery was, of course, under a plate which was held on by teeny screws. I needed a minuscule Phillips screwdriver, which we had, but where the hell was that at midnight in the rain, but in the shed, back outside and there were spiders out there. Loads of them, likely poisonous ones, and probably also snakes and opossums.

I found myself sobbing actual tears trying to make this monstrosity of a toy car stop playing. The music mocked me. It got louder and faster. It teased me by slowing so I thought it might stop, but then it honked a horn back to life and started all over again, but now a little off rhythm and a lot off key. It sounded like an ice cream truck driven by the murderous clowns from the urban legends that terrified us as children. And if that weren't enough, the unicorn began to whinny uncontrollably from the toy closet, as if begging to get out, except its once perky calls now sounded garbled, like the little lavender-maned mythical equine were both drunk AND drowning. Maniacal giggles preceded rasping, slow-motion shrieks of toy newborns, and the giggling doll drawled, in a voice that was uncharacteristically low, and utterly horrific:

"LET'S PLAY PEEKABOO!"

"DRINK, MAMAAAAAAAAAA."

"GOOOO TINKLE."

The plastic cat circled me like a shark.

"MEW."

"MEW."

Were this an actual *Twilight Zone* episode, the show would've ended here on a close-up of me screaming in abject terror while probably pulling out my hair while surrounded by haunted toys. Except this was real life, so it got worse.

The whole time I'd been praying the catastrophe wouldn't wake up my toddler, but naturally it did, so I had to leave the toy car, and the doll that peed, and the Duggar clan of crying doll babies, plus that rabid-assed plastic cat, and rock my sweet child back to sleep, which took at least a half hour because she kept asking me: "Car, Mama? Car? Ride the car?" All while I panicked and rocked and tried to figure out if I needed to call Ghost Hunters.

Anyone who's ever seen *Poltergeist* (pretty much the scariest movie of all time) is aware of the fact that toys can be terrifying, especially in the dark of night. There's something so uncanny about dolls and stuffed animals and any sort of childlike rendering of an adult thing. Given the right circumstances, toys can really creep you out, and that is exactly what had happened, and I'd let it get to me. I pride myself, however, on being a practical and rational human being (who has seen every episode of every ghost investigation show the Discovery Channel has ever aired) so I knew there was a logical explanation and absolutely nothing to fear, except a demonic legion of possessed playthings.

Finally, my daughter went back to sleep, and I mustered up enough courage to brave the shed in the middle of the night in gales of rain. I got the screwdriver and went back inside and through my frustrated tears I managed to unscrew the plate that held in the batteries. Wouldn't you know it that they were crusted in place and I had to get a knife to pry them out? It was like a miracle of silence when that damned thing shut up. I think I collapsed on the floor in a heap of gratitude for the quiet, for being rid of that awful organ-grinder circus of the macabre music.

And then I opened up the screen door and threw that car as far into the yard as I possibly could. You know, just in case it came back to life, which always happens in these kinds of stories, so I knew I needed to be prepared.

One by one, I turned off the other toys. I removed batteries, and stuffed dolls deep in the toy chest under heaps of blankets, just in case. I needed a good night's sleep after such trauma, and I didn't want to take any risks. I'd been through enough, and I'd take care of it in the morning.

Remember what I said about batteries? I bet you're wondering what this has to do with batteries, so let me explain.

Ghosts aren't real, and they don't take over our kids' toys. The demons in this story were debunked as low batteries. For reasons I have yet to understand, when the power runs down, electronic playthings take on a mind of their own, which results in their talking out of turn in spooky/drunk voices, and they tend to do this all at once because you got them all around the same time.

So, new parents? Unless you want to be like me and star in your own cheesy remake of *Child's Play*, I suggest you heed my warnings and stock up on batteries. Buy them in bulk, and make sure you change them often. If you don't want to listen to me, don't worry. I now give everyone a big box of double-As for their baby shower, and if I really like you, I'll throw in a few Ds and a Phillips screwdriver too.

*VICTORIA FEDDEN is the author of the memoir* This Is Not My Beautiful Life. *She lives with her family in Fort Lauderdale, Florida, and teaches writing at Palm Beach State College. She blogs on her website at* victoriafedden.com. *Visit her on Facebook.*

# Parents Catch ALL the Shit
## By Mike Cruse
### *Papa Does Preach*

My wife gives me constant crap because I don't listen to her, or something like that…I don't know, I'm usually not listening. But you know what, I'm okay with it, because here's the truth—she's right. Look, there's only so many stereotypes as a progressive man that I can try and break. But the whole "husband that doesn't listen" thing…yeah, sorry, that's me to a T.

I am your poster boy for idiot man when it comes to doing something I have my mind set on. And those are usually the cases when my wife tries to remind me I might screw something up, so maybe slow down, or pay a little more attention, or don't hang from the ladder by one foot while trying to reach an unreachable area in the house, or maybe don't light the grill looking into it when you know it's leaking gas.

Most of the time…a lot of the time…okay, some of the time, things work out in my favor, and I never miss an opportunity to say, "See, woman!! I know what I'm doing!!" which is always met with the predictable eye roll, and something about me not being so lucky next time, or, "Hey, how's that eyebrow growing back?"

But one place I knew I didn't need my wife's advice was when we had our second child. I mean come on, we just did this shit four years ago; I had this! I'd been killing it at this parent stuff for some time now. Well, maybe "killing it" is too strong, but I'm adequate, and my kid is alive, so back off.

So naturally, when our daughter was born, I went back into the ole storage facility in my noggin, found the box labeled "New Baby," and thumbed through some oldie-but-goodie info from when we did this whole rodeo the first time.

I knew we would have to do some of your standard baby stuff again, like eventually putting a safety gate back up and childproofing cabinets and outlets. But most of that stress-inducing first-time-parent stuff—I totally wasn't gonna waste my time on that again…my dad game was on point now. But that's when life has a funny of putting you in your place; humbling you to your very soul.

That moment came for me early on after our daughter arrived. This may sound weird, but I enjoy changing diapers. I know, not the sort of thing you hear from a dad, or anyone, really. I mean who enjoys being around all that shit? I guess it's kind of like that special moment for me. After you're done cleaning up your kids and putting their clean diaper back on, it's like you're sharing a moment together…a moment that is most times ruined instantly by more poop arriving.

Because I knew what I was doing, my diaper-changing skills being borderline pro status, I would always volunteer to change our little one. This would lead to my wife saying to me, "Hey, you should lay down a mat or something in case she poops again." To which she received my standard, "I got this, woman! This isn't my first rodeo. I don't need a mat."

The day of "the incident" was a day like any other. We were hanging out at home, enjoying the changing of the seasons, and being leisurely. Our daughter had woken up from a nap, so I retrieved her and took her over to the couch. After the customary goo-goos and gagas I decided to change her diaper before she fed. The wife, as always, said, "Hey…lay down a mat before you change her; you don't want her pooping on the couch," followed by my usual rebuffing of her advice and explanation of my awesome skills, which require no mat.

You know that point in a movie where a character is explaining their grand plan, or expressing how they have all the answers, and you know that person is gonna bite it really soon…yeah, that's the feeling I had right as I was finishing my statement of awesomeness to my wife, only to be greeted by my tiny daughter letting loose the most poop I have ever seen come out of a human being, let alone a seven-pounder. I mean, we're talking it's legitimately possible she was hooked up to a tube that was pumping nonstop poop out of it, into her butt, and then onto me. Sheer panic set in in that moment, and since I had nothing to shield the couch with, I instantly cupped my hands, full-on bowl style, and attempted to catch the shit in my hands.

Let me repeat that again, I CAUGHT…my daughter's shit…IN MY HANDS!! There I was, hands pushed together, like some poop-loving Oliver Twist asking my daughter's rear end, "Please, sir, may I have some more?" And her rear end was glad to oblige.

Now, I can't say for certain this was a planned hit, or that my daughter and wife somehow coordinated this event, but since the events of that day, I have noticed their relationship has grown by leaps and bounds.

So, the only advice I can impart on you men out there, especially those about to become dads: listen to your wife, because if you don't, one way or another, you're going to catch shit.

*MIKE CRUSE is the author and freelance writer behind the blog* Papa Does Preach. *Once he had lofty dreams to be a stand-up comedian or famous actor, but clearly didn't make enough poor life choices to get there, so now he just bugs people on the Internet. Mike's been named one of the funniest parents on the Internet from the likes of Buzzfeed,* The Huffington Post, *and the* TODAY Show; *even Hoda Kotb said he was one of her favorites of 2016. Born and raised in sunny San Diego, Mike now lives in Virginia with his wife and two children, because clearly he loves them, or why else would someone do that? Follow along at PapaDoesPreach.com as he fumbles his way through this whole parenting thing.*

# Adventures in Potty Training
## By Jorrie Varney
### *Close to Classy*

"What do you mean alligators live in the toilet?" she asked in wide-eyed terror.

My mother had made the somewhat catastrophic mistake of leaving me alone in the bathroom with my younger sister, who happened to be potty training at the time.

"Not just alligators, snakes, too, and those spiders that can run really fast across water. They live down in that hole at the bottom of the toilet," I lied.

The fear of having her pink parts chewed off by creatures of the deep became a bit of a hurdle in my sister's potty-training efforts. From that day on, convincing her to go near the toilet was a feat in itself, never mind getting her to actually sit on it.

Now, almost thirty years later, as a mother myself, I'm nearly certain this single lie was the birth of my potty-training karma.

Before becoming a parent, I'll admit, I didn't know much about teaching a kid to use the toilet. Social media had given me a false sense of confidence on the topic. Facebook seemed to be littered with photos and praise for toilet-trained tots. Like, thanks, girl from high school who I haven't seen in twenty years, for that lovely picture of your kid's morning dump.

Seriously, how hard could it be?

So, when it was time to potty train my first child, I opted for the three-day method. Why? Because, apparently, I hate myself and all my worldly possessions. More accurately, this was a recommended method from other parents—who, I now assume, are sadists. The selling point of this method is that all the magic happens in three days, and then you can get on with your urine-free life.

Here's what really happens: you spend two paychecks on character underwear, and then your kid spends three days peeing on everything you own. Oh, did I mention you get to set a timer and take the kid to the bathroom every twenty minutes? Because you do. Every twenty minutes, for *three* days.

Once you've depleted your confidence as a parent, and you're out of liquor, that's pretty much the end of the experiment. Or it was for me anyway, because my kid didn't make it to the potty even once. It was basically three days of golden showers for my furniture.

From that point forward, I completely ignored potty training. I didn't mention it, and if anyone else did, I flipped over a table and ran out of the room screaming. My kid was still in diapers, but I didn't care, eventually she would figure it out, and if she didn't, I would explain it to her at some point before college.

Now, I'm not saying avoidance is the answer, but a few months later, out of the blue, my kid asked to wear underwear, and another drop of urine never touched the floor. *Voila*, my kid was potty trained, and all was right in the world.

Then, I had another kid, and because our society thinks it's unacceptable to shit in the gutter like a feral cat, I had to potty train that one too.

Obviously, I planned to completely avoid the topic, because if it worked once before, why not again? Maybe this one would teach himself too. Unfortunately, he saw some of his friends using the potty and started asking questions. Thanks, Aiden, why don't you just tell him how fun street drugs are while you're at it?

Using the potty in a hit-and-miss fashion became our unintended routine. Sometimes my son would try, other times he didn't care. I went along with whatever he did, but was still pretty much avoiding involvement, unless I was forced to engage. This usually occurred when my son tried to remove his loaded diaper by himself. Anytime I saw him working on a steamy load, I stood by to head off a shitastrophy. This worked pretty well, until one day, it didn't.

I was in the bathroom brushing my teeth the morning it all went wrong.

Just as I was finishing up, my son walked into the bathroom, naked from the waist down. If you think that should have been a red flag, you obviously don't have children.

I began walking toward him, but was suddenly stopped dead in my tracks by the smell of disaster—and by disaster, I mean *shit*. That's when I saw it, a small brown smudge on the back of his hand, and then his wrist, and then OMG HOW DID YOU GET SHIT ON YOUR ELBOW?!

I tried to remain calm, but panic was setting in as I thought about his journey across the house wearing a pair of shittens. With my son in tow, I made my way toward the scene of the crime.

It was far more disturbing than what I'd envisioned. There was shit *everywhere*—on the wall, on the tub, the shower curtain, the sink, the cabinets, the faucet, the rug, and about 900 other surfaces between his bathroom and mine.

"I made a little bit of a mess," he said, peering down at his hands.

As I attempted to understand how he got it all over his hands, I watched in horror as he reached around and scratched an itch, dead center of his derriere, and the answer became obvious.

"This poop is pretty itchy," he said quizzically.

My first thought was fire. I'd just burn down the house; we could always rebuild. Sure, the hubs might be upset, and there's the whole "arson is illegal" thing, but this was an unprecedented amount of shit, any rational person would understand I had no other choice.

The threat of jail and half a bottle of wine convinced me to reconsider my options, and I decided it was probably best to just clean it up. I tried not to cry as I scrubbed the shit out from under my toddler's fingernails. Then, smudge by disgusting smudge, I cleaned up the rest of it.

The bleach fumes burned my eyes for three days, and I still have nightmares a few times a week, but somehow, we survived. Maybe, if I'd been a kinder, more sympathetic child I wouldn't have a shit-stained loveseat and a dog on anxiety medication. Perhaps karma would have been kinder.

If I could turn back time, I'd leave out all the stuff about alligators and sea snakes. Instead, I'd tell my baby sister the toilet is a magical vortex of wishes and dreams, much like tossing a penny in a fountain, your dreams come true with every deposit. But alas, here I am, the Baroness of Bleach, trudging through the eye of a literal shitstorm.

Here's hoping the worst is behind me, or at the very least, bleach is on sale this week.

*JORRIE VARNEY is a registered nurse and mother of two who writes about the reality and insanity of parenting on her blog* Close to Classy. *Her parenting style can best be described as Roseanne meets Mary Poppins. Jorrie's writing has been featured on platforms such as* Scary Mommy, TODAY Parents, *and* Sammiches and Psych Meds, *as well as many others.*

*She aspires to own furniture without stains and enjoy a shower without an audience. You can also find her on* Facebook *and* Instagram.

# Thrill Me
## By E. R. Catalano
### *Zoe vs. the Universe*

Most days, I'd prefer not to die. As far as daily goals go, I'd rank it top ten. But I don't think about dying every day. Most people don't. Or how could we concentrate on doing our taxes, brushing our teeth, or cleaning the litter box? None of those things would seem worth doing.

Though I may not consciously think of death, I'm also not jumping out of any airplanes. When people talk of wild, daring thrill seekers, my name does not come up. I like quiet thrills. The unexpected dip in the road, a scary movie, a new book arriving in the mail. I know that a lot of this stems from anxiety and, since becoming a mom, my wish for my daughter to be less anxious and more daring than I am is at odds with my wish for her safety.

When she was a toddler, I followed a friend's advice to let her explore without hovering over her. This was supposed to help her establish independence and become less fearful. So I'd stand back and if (when) she got hurt, I'd pause before I reacted, since my friend's further advice was: "Don't show you're upset and maybe she won't get upset either since she'll look to you for signs."

This part wasn't too hard. I have a reputation for being calm in a crisis. My calm is deceptive though. For one thing, I'm good at hiding my emotions. For another, I have little to no situational awareness.

I walk through the world unaware of possible dangers because I have a tendency to get stuck in my head. I worry over unlikely threats like, what if that weird pimple on my face is the beginning of elephant man disease? Or what if my daughter flunks out of college? (She's currently in first grade.) Or what if she becomes a business major? (Nothing against business majors, but what will she and I talk about if she doesn't major in the humanities?!) I'd be so preoccupied with hypothetical worry over future estrangement from my hedge-fund-managing daughter that I'd trip over a tree branch, or I wouldn't notice the man waving the box cutter who was causing the rest of the commuters to move to my end of the subway car. Finally I'd look up, thinking, *What is it with these people?* just as the train pulled into the next station, and the doors opened, and everyone ran off. Including Box Cutter Guy.

Then my slowness to react masquerades as brilliance as I remain in my seat, safe, alone, a whole train car to myself during rush hour. Ah, a silent background for my thoughts! Where was I? Oh yes, could the mole on my elbow be cancer?

Besides being naturally averse to risk, I haven't had much opportunity. In my youth I was straitlaced and bookish. Though I was involved in a brawl in a nightclub once. This is so out of character that it's a story I like to polish then bring out and present to folks from time to time to give myself the veneer of "having lived."

No one buys it.

Obviously I'm not advocating bar fights for six-year-olds, but I'd like my daughter to be wise enough to know it's okay to be a little unwise from time to time.

Therefore, since she came into my life I've often wrestled with the question of when I should push her to try new, scary things and when I should sit back and let her grow at her own pace. I've read countless articles favoring one approach or the other. Then my friend/advisor said, "You know your own child best," which was a nice vote of confidence but also terrifying. Do you really know someone just because they lived inside your abdomen for a time?

What I do know is my daughter's history of bravery is sketchy. She can be a daredevil, but only if she doesn't have time to think about the possible consequences. If she does have time to think, and there's a chance she'll get hurt, she's not going to do whatever the thing is, just like her mom.

The first time she slid down a fireman's pole at a park was also the last, at least for a long while.

That first time she didn't think she could get hurt, until after she slid down and realized how quickly the ground—hard and covered in poky things—had approached. Even though she'd been fine, that thought, the possibility of getting hurt, got stuck in her head. Me again!

I decided to push—though I called it "encourage"—and so for months I stood at the bottom of that pole and "helped her slide," which basically meant getting her shoes in my face as she scooted her butt off the edge a millimeter at a time until I was able to reach up and lift/catch her. No one's definition of a slide, but good for the definition of my triceps. Eventually I gave up and stopped mentioning it, until one day she slid down on her own. Score one for "own pace."

Which brings me to last summer, when I decided to introduce my daughter to roller coasters, the one area where I felt I was wild and daring. I hadn't been on a roller coaster in several years, and I couldn't wait to see if she also loved the stomach-dropping falls, the sudden violent turns, and the breakneck speeds as much as I did.

At the amusement park, we tried the tamest roller-coaster-type ride first: the log flume. After all, who could be afraid of the log flume?

One guess.

While we were in line she saw the only drop. And she did not like it. Then, as we got closer to the front of the line, she saw how wet people were by the end of the ride and that was it. I let her get off the line, saying to myself "own pace." This became my mantra as we abandoned line after line due to her misgivings. Her "own pace" was turning out to be just as frustrating as "pushing."

Finally, she chose a type of ride I'd never given a second glance. It had four rocket ships—the one she liked was painted pink with a face painted on it—that just went really high and then around and around. Seemed boring. We got on, and when the ride began and our ship rose in the air and started to spin, I revised my opinion to: seems deadly.

I'd somehow never realized I was afraid of heights. They say knowledge is power, but I say that that power is fear. My daughter had no fear because she didn't know what could go wrong. She implicitly trusted our anthropomorphized rocket ship. That old, rickety, and, for all I knew, poorly maintained machine. She trusted the pin holding the gate closed, the one rattling and shaking in its holder as we spun around 100 feet above the hard and poky ground, wouldn't suddenly come loose, causing the gate to yawn wide, and centripetal force wouldn't be enough to keep us from hurtling out and down, down, splat.

"Close your eyes if you're scared," I said to her, my own eyes squeezed shut.

"But then I can't see. Look, Mommy, you can see the whole park."

I opened one eye. And my stomach flipped.

Thankfully we made it back to earth safely, and she wanted to go on again, much to my horror. But I swallowed my fear and followed my own advice to push myself. How else could I grow?

Before we left that day, I did go on a roller coaster, all by myself. This time knowledge would've helped. Specifically, the knowledge that as you age, the fluid in your inner ear lessens or changes or something (I'm not an ear scientist!) and you're less able to deal with sudden violent shifts in altitude or direction.

For the two whole minutes I was on that roller coaster, experiencing the stomach-dropping falls, the sudden violent turns, and the breakneck speed, I was terrified, nauseated, and my head felt like it was going to come off. I really thought I was going to die. But again, following my own advice, I didn't.

*E. R. CATALANO is a writer and mother of one evil mastermind living in Brooklyn, New York. She writes a humor blog at* www.zoevstheuniverse.com, *and she's a contributor to the previous title in this series,* I Just Want to Be Perfect, *as well as* The Bigger Book of Parenting Tweets *and* Never Will I Ever (and Then I Had Kids). *Her writing has also appeared on* McSweeney's, Scary Mommy, MockMom, *and* HaHas for HooHas, *among others. She has a novel-in-progress called* Becoming the Girl Detective *as well as a collection of stories called* Prove You're Not a Robot. *You can follow her on Facebook and on Twitter at @zoevsuniverse. She needs all the validation she can get.*

# Five Contemporary Alternatives to Nagging
## By Katia Bishops
### *IAMTHEMILK*

Everyone knows how much moms enjoy nagging. It's probably their second favorite thing in the world after personalized wake-ups by their first-favorite-thing-in-the-world (hint: not a generic, tardy alarm clock).

Moms are old and they still remember things like the '90s and the term "clash of civilizations" (which does not refer to Minecraft). They find themselves mentally reverting to that term every time they try to talk so kids will listen but kids won't, because duh, nagging is only fun for moms.

As if they've never heard the definition of "insanity," moms keep repeating the sentence "put your socks on" over and over again expecting the result to be different.

Things have changed since the '90s and just because your parents were nagging and using a modem doesn't mean you should. How about switching it up a little, Mom? Below are several suggestions to help you get better traction the next time you pitch an idea to your kids.

### Try a little mindfulness

The '90s were all about angst, grunge, and over-plucking your eyebrows. The oughts are about mindfulness. You can't swing a dead cat without hitting someone who's consciously breathing through something. Mindfulness is everywhere. We breathe on the yoga mat to remind ourselves to be in our bodies and in the present. We buy our kids books to teach them how to live in the moment because we all know how kids can get so wrapped up in the past and obsess about the future.

What would a mindful approach to "put your socks on" look like? It's always about being in the moment. Really be that person asking that other person to put their socks on and sit with that feeling for a while. (That part should be easy.) Your kids will probably elect another moment to be in, but at least you'll get to work on your mindfulness muscle during an intense (half-hour minimum guaranteed) practice session.

Your presentation sucks. Have you considered updating your elevator pitch or signing up for Toastmasters?

Yes, you've landed the gig of a lifetime (literally), and yes, your employers are four and seven years old, but it doesn't mean you should stop striving to impress them just because the job is yours (your attitude sucks, BTW)! If you're going to always be selling (product: socks; concept: basic hygiene/ceasefire; fantasy: sleep), then you'll need to perfect your pitch. Even a preschooler can tell your current (PowerPoint-less, I might add) presentation is not only boring but quite frankly a bit disturbing.

Have you ever had to sit through a presentation where the speaker repeated the same recommendation fifteen times using the same tone only to unexpectedly lash out at you on the sixteenth round as if you're to blame for their monotonous delivery? Who does that?

Friendly reminder: Look around you, Mom. Nobody's headbanging here (okay, that might be an alternative fact) and you are not Nirvana performing "Smells Like Teen Spirit." Please stop all that yelling!

Snapchat it

I'm not exactly sure how to Snapchat "put your sock on" (or anything else), but I've heard enough OF Snapchat to know it provides access to fawn snouts and flower garlands to those seeking them. Maybe fawn snouts and flower garland filters are your kids' thing, you never know.

Buy a Hawaiian flower necklace at the Dollar Store, spray-paint it to give it that dreamy filtery hue, and then wrap it around your children's socks a couple of times. When you hand it over, make sure to hashtag your request like so: hashtag put your socks on!

## Netflix it

You may be going, "Pardon me? How do I Netflix 'put on your socks'?" I'm sorry to hear you're so out of touch with the via moderna. Let me tech support you through this:

1. Go to create profiles.
2. Add new.
3. Name it "Put Your Socks On."
4. Better yet, change your kid's existing profile name to that. You know you want to.

### Find and harness your inner coach

You've probably noticed nowadays everyone harbors an inner coach, or at the very least an inner non-certified consultant. If you don't believe me just read **The Life-Changing Magic of Tidying Up** written by Marie Kondo, Japan's leading Tidy Up Consultant, and never be surprised again in your life.

To get certified as a coach you'll need to pay a lot of money and temporarily transition your Netflix watching rights and time slot to Put Your Socks On in order to clear up your own schedule (meaning that one hour of me time) in order to take those online courses. The bang for your buck will make it worth your while. You will get to add three letters to your name on your LinkedIn profile and more importantly you will know everything.

Including how to convince your child to put their socks on.

*KATIA BISHOPS is the creator of* IAMTHEMILK, *a Wordpress-recommended blog in the family category (2014-2015). Katia spent thirty years wanting to write and making excuses for not doing it. It took immigration and a challenging second pregnancy to start (don't try this at home). Since she started blogging in 2012, Katia was part of* Redbook *magazine's blogger team, Netflix's StreamTeam, and her writing was featured on multiple websites and in print.*

*Katia is a mother of two who must have done something really bad in her previous life which she is paying for now by not sleeping. She channels her frustration via memes on her Facebook page and her creativity via Instagram.*

# What Doesn't Kill You Makes You Stronger
## By Linda Wolff
### *Carpool Goddess*

I didn't always try to get myself killed. It only began when I had kids.

Sitting in a power boat on a tranquil lake while the sun shines gloriously above sounds lovely, picturesque even, unless you have a harness strapped between your legs strangling your lady bits and shoving your breasts into a cleavage situation impossible even by the nuclear feats of the latest Victoria's Secret push-up bra.

There was a moment there I could actually rest my chin comfortably on my own rack.

But then the captain floored it and the honeymoon was over. My body was heaved into the air with a yank that rattled my ovaries.

"Mommies do brave things too..." I yelled, my voice fading into the distance. My parachute filling with air.

"What?" shouted the kids as they got smaller and smaller.

Feeling like I had been shot out of a cannon and certain I was on the verge of cardiac arrest, I waved frantically for the young captain to bring me back down. So much for proving mommies can do brave things too.

"Look, Mommy's waving!" my daughter said, thrusting her small undulating arms high in the air.

"Hi, Mommy!" shouted my son. His arms mimicking my SOS.

"She sure looks like she's having fun." The sadistic captain smiled, giving a generous wave.

"Are they doing a fucking wave?!" I fumed, trying to yank the harness out of my crotch.

What you don't know is I'm deathly afraid of heights. And being catapulted hundreds of feet into the air, at breakneck speed, on the back of a speedboat, by my nether regions is top on my list of things NEVER TO DO. Only second to "Don't jump out of an airplane."

Having a panic attack while in mid-air, while doing the thing you swore you would never do, is something you can never fully prepare for. Nothing like a little cardiac arrhythmia to top off a perfectly blissful day.

Once my breathing finally calmed, I promised myself that if I survived I would tell everyone I tried parasailing twice.

It would be my first and last time.

As I mentioned earlier, I didn't always try to get myself killed. It only began when I had kids.

You see, my husband and I are complete opposites.

He's big and strapping and sporty and coordinated and fearless.

And, well, I'm klutzy, fearful, and prone to dizzy spells. And if you count the assessment of the junior high assistant gymnastics teacher, a "total spaz."

My husband practically grew up whooshing down icy white mountains at supersonic speeds and defying gravity by gliding on smooth lakes with nothing but a rope and two little skis.

I have a hard enough time balancing on my own two feet on solid ground. How in the world can I compete with that?

I can't.

I have a fear of heights. A fear of tight spaces. And a fear of dying a horrible death from one of the above.

He's fearless and I want my kids to be like him, not like me.

"Daddy can do anything," my kids swoon. "He's A-MAY-ZING."

Yeah, I know.

I've spent most of my kids' childhoods trying to prove that daddies aren't the only ones who are athletic and brave. I've tried to do A-MAY-ZING things too.

At my dear husband's encouragement—"I don't want you missing out on all the fun."

"Fun for who?" I asked. I pushed myself to learn how to ski so my kids would see that Mommy didn't completely suck at doing physical stuff.

I should have known better.

Just getting the kids dressed in the billions of layers that little kids need and then have to peel off five minutes later, because they have to pee, was a workout. I was exhausted before I even left the hotel room.

It doesn't matter that I never graduated from the bunny slopes. To my kids, the bunny slope looked impressively steep. And that's good enough for me.

But even my modest accomplishment didn't feel like anything to celebrate when my husband could magically ski down the hill backward saying, "Ski to Daddy." They think he's a superhero.

What I didn't realize then was that hopping on the back of a sled and sliding down a puny-sized hill or just putting extra marshmallows in their hot chocolate could have made me their hero too.

I was so fixated with worry that my son would grow up thinking girls didn't do bold things, and that my daughter would think she couldn't do them either, that I made myself miserable trying to prove what they may or may have not even been thinking was wrong. You can see how futile this is, right?

What my kids don't know is I faced my greatest fear just stepping onto the airplane to get to the effing mountain vacation. Or that the reason I hum to myself while on the chairlift is not to entertain them, but so I don't completely lose my shit because I'm dangling in midair by one thin cable. Now that's bravery! But that stuff goes right over their precious little heads.

No, they want to see you do A-MAY-ZING stuff. Bold and fearless like a cartoon character.

And, after all these years I'm done trying. I only wish I would have figured this out earlier.

It all started when my young daughter pointed her dainty arm toward her dad and big brother while they floated under parachutes in the sky, and said, yet again, "Only boys do stuff like that."

Something in me snapped and the next thing you know, I was up, up, and away too. Tethered to the back of a boat by my groin.

So I have forced myself to do things. Things that make me very uncomfortable. All for the sake of teaching my precious offspring that girls can do anything boys can do.

And it's almost killed me a few times.

Like the time I went skiing with my husband and kids and found myself at the top of a mountain and a snowboarder came careening toward us, completely out of control, as we stood at the start of a steep hill. My husband didn't see the wayward teen and began his descent down the slippery white slope. A bloodcurdling scream came from my throat. "Louis!" He turned and stopped.

"Catch the kids," I yelled, and with gentle shoves to their backs my kids began gliding down the hill toward the V of their dad's big open arms.

"WEE!" they squealed.

Unfortunately, I didn't have time to save myself. And WHAM!

Thank God my ample rump proved helpful and worked like an anchor, keeping me from being catapulted headfirst down the icy hill. But there was some collateral damage: The snowboarder's fist found my cheek as she landed.

"Don't worry, I'm fine!" I muffled through a mouth full of gauze as the ski patrol loaded me onto their sled.

"Can we ride on the big red sled too?" asked my blissfully innocent kids as the patrol whisked me down the hill.

"No, that's just for Mommy. They don't want her bleeding on the mountain."

"Ew."

Don't think I didn't give the idiot snowboarder a piece of my mind. Good thing the kids were out of earshot, or they would have learned a slew of new words they couldn't use on the playground. But the true idiot was me.

The things I did to prove I was something that I wasn't seem ridiculous to me now.

I have no idea what I was thinking. Would they like me more? Think I was cool? If I really wanted to prove that girls play sports I could have just turned on the TV and let them watch the Olympics. What a crock of shit I dumped on myself for trying to be everything. For thinking I had to be perfect.

What I learned, because hindsight is 20/20, after all: Fearlessness can be manifested in many ways. It doesn't have to be at breakneck speed while careening down a mountain. Or hundreds of feet up at heart attack level. It's showing courage and bravery when facing problems or our fears. Dealing with those suckers head-on.

The fact that I have an aversion to heights, risk, and sweat doesn't mean I'm not bold or capable. There are things I'm good at that my husband is not. We show our fearlessness in different ways. I'm not afraid to try to whip up something new in the kitchen, while the mere handling of Tupperware gives him hives. Or pull out wiggly teeth like a dental ninja, impervious to the sight of blood. Or go back to school to get a degree when I'm old enough to be my fellow students' mother. I could go on and on.

I don't need to be a carbon copy of my husband or any man, or any other woman, for that matter.

There were plenty of moms who at the ski lodge happily read and sipped cocoa (or stronger stuff) by a roaring fire who seemingly didn't feel one ounce of guilt for not braving the mountain with their kids like I did. I might have even judged them at the time. But I was jealous and in awe of their confidence and self-awareness and the slack they cut for themselves. Truth is I wanted to be them. Someone who doesn't need to prove shit to anyone.

And now that I've given up extreme sports, my kids are just as happy playing in the pool with their dear old mom, because I'm the parent who loves to be in the water for hours on end. I can't fall in there and I can't feel myself sweat. It doesn't get much better than that. And when I hear them have to beg their dad to come in the pool, well, it gives me a little thrill.

What? I never said I was perfect.

*LINDA WOLFF writes at* Carpool Goddess, *where she proves that midlife, motherhood, and the empty nest aren't so scary.* TODAY Parents *called her one of the funniest parents on Facebook, and her humorous essays have been published in numerous anthologies. Her work has been featured on* The Washington Post, The Huffington Post, Good Housekeeping, Cosmopolitan, Scary Mommy,

TODAY Parents, Grown and Flown, Babble, *and more. She lives in Los Angeles with her husband and is the proud mama of two grown kids. Follow her on Facebook, Instagram, and Twitter. You know you want to.*

# It's Tricky

## Susanne Kerns

### *The Dusty Parachute*

Growing up as a goofy-looking kid with Coke-bottle glasses and headgear can lead you down one of two paths in life. There's the one where you have parents who recognize and accept your reality and temper your expectations for your future. Or, there's the one where your mom overcompensates for your shortcomings by constantly reassuring (brainwashing) you that you are beautiful and perfect, while limiting your access to mirrors and other reflective surfaces.

This is also the same mom who insists you can "be anything you want to be" if you put your mind to it. It only took me until seventh-grade cheerleading tryouts to discover this was total bullshit.

Okay, maybe it wasn't so much bullshit as I could have used some more clarity around what "putting your mind to it" entailed. She probably meant "put your mind to it" in the "dedicate yourself to acquiring the skills needed to achieve a certain goal" way, which when you think of it, really isn't putting your mind to it, so much as your time, energy, and body to it. That sounds like an awful lot of work.

Instead, I took the statement literally and "put my mind to it" by simply thinking a lot about how much I wanted it. You know, like in that book *The Secret*, where you visualize your way to making your dreams a reality? I visualized myself wearing the cute little cheerleading skirt with the alternating blue-and-white pleats, the Lotto tennis shoes with mix-and-match multicolored Velcro hashtags on the sides, and the sweater with the big Bullpup patch on the back. If only *The Secret* had been around in 1985, I would have dream-boarded the hell out of that cheerleading uniform and manifested it right into my reality.

Unfortunately, I was so wrapped up in my "you can do anything you put your mind to" attitude that I missed several signs I was not nailing the cheerleading tryouts process.

First, there was the dance competition. Unlike all my friends who had entire shelves dedicated to gymnastics trophies and dance recital photos featuring satin bodysuits, bedazzled with sequins, my only award was for watching the most consecutive VHS-taped episodes of *Days of Our Lives*. Not surprisingly, my extensive knowledge of Marlena Evans and Victor Kiriakis's backstory did not benefit me in any way when trying to figure out what a "ball change" or "chassé" was.

Adding to the challenge of memorizing the dance moves were the questionable lyrics of the song we were performing the dance to: "It's Tricky" by Run-DMC.

*"I met this little girlie, her hair was kinda curly."*

Hey, that sounds like me!

*"Went to her house and bust her out, I had to leave real early."*

Should I know what "bust her out" means?

*"These girls are really sleazy, all they just say is please me."*

Okay. Even by 1986 standards, this is pretty bad.

The final stage of cheerleading tryouts was the interview portion where we were judged on our poise. Like our dance song, this portion was also "tricky," mostly because I did not know what the word "poise" meant. Based on the ninth-grade cheerleader who conducted the interview, my best guess was that poise meant "being a big ol' bitch."

I don't recall how poised I was, because, like in all one-on-one interview situations, I experienced a complete anxiety-induced, autopilot trance. Maybe I did a solo performance of the "It's Tricky" dance for her. Maybe I told her how poise-y I thought she and all her friends were. I most likely rambled for ten minutes about how I wished I was one of the Wakefield twins from Sweet Valley High before collapsing into the fetal position, rocking in a corner while I told her how pretty her hair was.

Because it was 1986, a decade before adults started considering the long-term psychological impact their poor decisions could have on kids, our school chose to announce the cheerleader winners in a way that maximized job security for an entire generation of therapists: one by one, at a school dance. Yes, you heard me right. A public display of winners and losers, right in the middle of a mother f-ing middle school dance.

My mom dropped me off, dressed in my finest matching Esprit ensemble. About an hour into the dance, the DJ stopped the music and handed a microphone to the captain of the cheerleading squad to announce the newest additions to the team. I stood, full of misguided confidence, while my friends were called, one by one, to go stand at the front of the dance floor with the other chosen ones. As each name was called, I concentrated all my mental energy into hoping my name would be read next, until there was no next.

Certainly they must have misplaced the slip of paper with my name on it. After all, I had put my mind to it so hard! My mom said I can do anything I put my mind to, dammit!

The DJ started the next song. Let's say it was Simple Minds's "Don't You Forget About Me," because that's the only song that could possibly capture the pure John Hughes-middle-school-soul-crushing-ness of this moment. Except, I wasn't even the Molly Ringwald in this scene. I was more like Molly's even more awkward sister who you only see in passing in family photos in the background since she was sent to live at a boarding school for girls who can't do toe-touches or herkie jumps.

Instead of being poised and having the grace and dignity to congratulate my excited friends, I went the "big ol' bitch" route and ran to the nearest pay phone to do what any girl who just had all her hopes and dreams destroyed would do....call my mom to ask her to come pick me up.

She came to my rescue quickly and I spent the next few hours mastering my face-in-the-pillow soul cry, as only a mid-puberty girl can. My mom patiently stayed with me, alternating between hugs and back rubs, depending on my crying position.

Somewhere between my tearful gasps for air and trumpeting nose blows, my mom shared the words of wisdom that have held true and got me through many rough patches in the past thirty years. She told me that even though it seemed impossible to imagine now, things would work out and I should get some sleep because everything always looks better in the morning.

Sure enough, through forty years of cheating boyfriends, breakups, fights with friends, shitty days at work, quitting jobs, waiting for test results, school wait lists for my kids, and even the loss of beloved friends and family, no matter how dark things seem at night, things always look better the next morning.

And despite my lazy, teenage interpretation of her original words of wisdom, I have also found over the years that you really can do most anything you put your mind to, as long as your mind tells you to get your ass in gear and start taking action without giving up instead of just sitting around thinking about how much you want it.

There are no shortcuts to getting what you want in life and there's no "secret" for wishing things into reality. In the wise words of Run-DMC, *"It's like that y'all (y'all), but we don't quit. You keep on (rock!) shock! 'cause this is it."*

It's tricky, tricky, tricky.

*SUSANNE KERNS is a writer and marketing consultant living in Austin, Texas, with her husband and two children whom she lovingly refers to as the "11-year-old" and "7-year-old." Her stories have been featured in the books,* I Just Want to Be Perfect, It's Really 10 Months - Special Delivery, *and* Martinis & Motherhood: Tales of Wonder, Woe & WTF?! *as well as a variety of websites, including her blog,* The Dusty Parachute.

*Follow her on Facebook to see why she's frequently featured on* TODAY *Parents "Funniest Parents on Facebook" roundup. She's also on Instagram, where she posts her tasteful nudes.\* (\*Mostly photos of poorly lit food, and animals, all nude.) You can also find her on Twitter whenever she accidentally opens the wrong app on her phone.*

# The Terrible T.E.E.N.S.
## (Troublesome, Evil, Exasperating, and Narcissistic Spawn)
## By Rodney Lacroix

The "Terrible Twos"?

Bitch, please.

I submit, for your approval, that the "Terrifying Teens" make the "Terrible Twos" look like a restful vacation watching nuns picking daisies from white puffy clouds while sitting in a hammock on a beach during a sunny day in Hawaii.

I have four children in total. I have two biological children and two stepchildren, ranging in ages from eight years old to sixteen.

I've lived through the Terrible Twos so many times that I have a Rewards Card. However, when you get your Terrible Twos Rewards Card stamped they do it with a dirty diaper while you try to calm your child down in a restaurant. Why did you bring your toddler to a restaurant? Do you hate other people, or are you just hoping they share in your misery?

I was a conscientious parent and didn't take my children out to a restaurant until they learned to stop crying in public. Most of them were at least in middle school before they ever tried their first blooming onion.

If you're reading this and you're planning on bringing your crying baby to a restaurant, just know everyone in there hates you.

Where was I?

Oh. Teens.

My biological children are the oldest of the four kids. My son, who is scarily just like me except he's four inches taller and doesn't have a bald spot big enough to sell ad space on, is thirteen years old. My daughter, who shares my love for roller coasters, rock and roll, and being angry at everyone for no reason, is sixteen. The fact that they actually reached those ages given their propensity for driving me insane is a testament to my own tried-and-true philosophy of always having noise-canceling headphones and a cold bottle of beer nearby.

The teenage years, though. These are tough times to be a parent. They get even tougher when the prospect of one of them driving an automobile comes along.

But, first, some backstory and history on the plight of being a teen's parent.

Prior to becoming teenagers, kids become something known as a "tween." Tweens did not exist when I was a child. Our growing phases pretty much went from baby to toddler to annoying as shit to young adult to teenager. That was our progression. Nowadays, the "annoying as shit" and "young adult" phases have been combined to form something called a "tween" as in "you're in beTWEEN being a little a-hole and a big a-hole."

Tween years are okay because nothing is really happening. Your kids are just, there. They're almost like pets that have to do homework. Sometimes these pets require you to help them figure out things like algebra or maybe build a diorama that you really got screwed on by the stupid teacher who only gave it a B-minus even after you spent $53 of your own money on it and did most of the project yourself and even HANDPAINTED THE JAGUARS THAT YOU DEFTLY FORMED OUT OF MODELING CLAY. WTF.

Tween years are bitter years for many a parent.

However, when you have a girl tween, this also means that they are in the phase of "becoming a woman." This is an entirely disgusting process I will not describe here but, suffice it to say, you may be required to run out to a pharmacy to buy things you really don't want to.

After the tween years come the teen years.

This is when things really start to suck for parents.

My son currently grows at a rate of three feet per month. By the time you finish this story, he will have grown two-and-a-half inches and will be sporting no less than forty-seven new armpit hairs. In my experience, though, boys are *way* easier to raise than girls, so all we really need to do for my son is keep him hydrated and move him away from his Xbox to a sunny spot near the window every few days and he's good to go.

My teenage daughter, though.

Teenage girls have boyfriends (or girlfriends) and problems and issues and these things called "moments" where if you say the wrong thing—no matter how right you think it is—they will hate and despise you for up to thirty minutes. Then they will emerge from their bedroom as if nothing ever happened, leaving you to wonder if you'd just imagined the whole episode. That is until you say something like, "Hey—" at which point said teenage girl will burst into tears and lock herself in her room again. This repeats in thirty-minute cycles for three years until they turn sixteen and can then just leave the house and take off in the car.

Ah. The car. Now we've come full circle to the crux of the matter.

My daughter, you see, is in the process of testing for her driver's license. I live in New Hampshire, so getting a driver's license simply involves taking your moose to town while wearing a new pair of cutoff jean shorts and being able to describe the fall foliage in detail. Wait, I'm getting confused with Vermont. Never mind.

In New Hampshire, teens can start driving at age fifteen and a half without a permit, as long as there is someone twenty-five years or older in the car. Luckily for me, the local retirement home lets you take elderly people out for the day, so I'd usually prop one of them up in the passenger seat, buckle the old guy in, and then tell my daughter to be back in an hour for bingo.

New Hampshire state law requires each teen has forty hours of parent-supervised driving time and ten hours of instructor-supervised driving time.

Yes. The instructors *who are supposed to be teaching the teens how to drive* get to be in the car 75 percent less than I do.

Seems legit.

I've had six accidents and 540 speeding tickets in all my years of driving so, sure, let's have the kids spend more time in a car with me. Makes sense. When you see articles of people hitting the gas instead of the brake and driving through buildings, there's a decent chance someone like me had to supervise forty hours of that person's driving time.

I can tell you, honestly, that sitting in a car with a teenager for forty hours is an exercise in patience and mental stamina and how well you do suppressing your own heart failure. If you have children and are used to raising your voice at them because they're doing something wrong like breaking things or spilling things or leaving things out or shaving the dog, then supervising a teenager's driving may not be right for you.

It's terrifying.

I once lost my son in my own house when he was two years old. I forget what I was doing—most likely singing along with my daughter to *The Wiggles*—(HELL YEAH, FRUIT SALAD IS YUMMY YUMMY)—but I remember looking down and my son was no longer there beside me. He had crawled off somewhere that was not within my immediate vicinity. I remember always wanting my babies to start talking and walking but in hindsight, most parents now know that is a really stupid thing to wish for. Once a kid starts talking he doesn't stop. And once a baby starts crawling you spend the majority of your time trying to get him to stop getting to where he's going before he barrels down the stairs or pulls over a dresser or thinks the dog's tail looks delicious.

My son was gone. I ran frantically around the house and finally stopped at the base of our stairs leading to our new, unfinished second floor. There, on the very edge of the balcony above me, sat my son. He had crawled away and up the stairs and had propped himself on the very edge of the second-floor hallway that did not have a railing installed yet. You can imagine my terror looking up at him, sitting on the edge of the balcony over my head, as I prayed he didn't fall. He didn't fall, but I certainly had to change my own diaper after that one.

The dread you feel while driving with a teenager is similar to the kind in that scene, but now the scene has changed. Now the baby is teetering on the edge of a roof and is also dancing while the roof is icy and there are alligators on the ground. There are also giant spiders riding the alligators and everything is made of lava. So, it's like the original balcony scene times a thousand billion.

When you're a parent and your child is driving you around in a 4,000-pound vehicle, sitting there in that passenger seat and giving that child complete control over both your lives is horrific. What I always take for granted now seems so difficult to teach.

Look at the road signs.

Use your directional.

Turn your head before you change lanes.

You need a phone charger in this car because my phone is almost dead and I need to live-tweet this.

Maintain space between cars.

Hands at eight and four positions.

Seriously, we need a car charger in here because I'm at, like, 28 percent battery.

I've never been a patient person. I live in New England so we are used to swearing and flipping off everyone in other cars simply as a neighborly gesture. But sitting on that passenger side and surrendering all of yourself to your child is something else entirely. In those forty hours of driving with my daughter, I learned how to trust her judgment and remain calm in allowing her to handle the situation. I've learned not to interject every thirty seconds and let her learn from her own mistakes, as long as the mistake wouldn't result in us rear-ending a logging truck and ending up as a Fox News story that begins with the word "Tragic."

I also learned that pushing down on an imaginary brake pedal for forty hours is a really fantastic workout for your core.

By the time you read this, I'm sure my daughter will have her license and be driving around. I can't imagine my anxiety watching her drive away on her own for the very first time. I'm sure it will feel a lot like that time I found him sitting up on that balcony.

Speaking of my son, he just reminded me he'll be eligible to drive in just under two years.

Ah. There they are. The real Terrible Twos.

*RODNEY LACROIX is best known as a humorist and author of* several bestselling comedy books. *His tweets and posts on various social media sites have appeared on Buzzfeed,* TODAY Show, *and* The Huffington Post. *Rodney's books have won him multiple humor awards, including a medal for his first book which he refuses to take off and, honestly, is starting to smell.*

*Rodney lives in southern New Hampshire. He is a husband to a wife way hotter than he deserves, proud biological father of two amazing children, and step-ological father of two step-amazing stepchildren. He also likes to invent terms.*

*You can find Rodney Lacroix on* Amazon, Facebook, Twitter, *and* RodneyLacroix.com. *You can't miss him. He's the one wearing the stinky gold medal.*

*One final note: Rodney's daughter did pass her driver's license test and is currently terrorizing the roads of New Hampshire. We suggest you lock yourselves indoors just to be safe.*

# That Time I Died in Checkout Lane Number 3
## By Sarah Cottrell
### *Housewife Plus*

Like most decent parents, I publicly ignore my parenting faults and broadcast my achievements and all those soft and fuzzy feelings of how sweet I think my kids are. It just isn't exactly a smart etiquette choice to brag about how your toddler knows where the beer is kept or that Mom and Dad walk around in their underwear some Sunday mornings. We keep that shit private like everyone else.

But sometimes, no matter how hard you try to contain the slip-ups and the doozies that befall even the most disciplined of parents, there will come a moment of reckoning when your child outs your imperfect parenting ass in a very public way.

Like that Thursday my kid outed me.

It was quitting time at work and my husband and the kids were on their way to pick me up. They called me to let me know they had just arrived and I grabbed my bag and jacket and headed out the door. I work in the heart of downtown where at 5:00 p.m. traffic can get a little bonkers. After climbing into the car, buckling my seat belt, and fielding instantaneous requests for me to download new games on the kids' tablets, I looked over at my husband and saw a familiar grimace on his face. He was trying not to swear out loud at the idiot drivers in the next lane over.

In an effort to keep the peace before Dad was ready to blow his top at other drivers, I quickly turned around and said, "Hey, kids, I was thinking we'd swing by the grocery store and get some stuff to make homemade pizzas. How does that sound?" My seven-year-old son,

Barley, looked up from Minecraft to ask if we could get some pepperoni this time, and of course I huffed some mom-style negotiation about including a vegetable. He shouted back, "But Mom! Why do you always say—?"

And this is a pivotal moment here, folks. You see, my son got cut off by my husband, whose forehead vein was in full throb mode as he snarled out a quick, "Stay in your lane, asshole!" My eyebrows went up at the same time as the shrill in my voice as I gave him a sharp, "Hey!" My husband, realizing there were young ears in the car and now an unimpressed wife looked into the rearview and apologized, "Sorry, everyone! No one should ever talk like that! My apologies!"

A few short miles and quick right turn later, we were pulling into the parking lot.

Generally, when we go to the grocery store, one of us stays in the car with the kids and the other makes a mad dash to pick up whatever thing we stopped for. Our kids can get crazy loud and have a dreadful habit of picking fights with each other. What kids don't though?

We pulled into a spot in the nearly full parking lot and spent five minutes arguing with the kids about why we were not going to take the race car-shaped cart from the family three cars down; that just wasn't nice.

Once in the store, we experienced an exceedingly painful walk through one aisle while the kids bickered and moaned about "wanting this and not wanting that, pizza is gross, no, it isn't, how come he always gets to sit in the cart and I have to walk" nonsense. Not feeling an overwhelming urge to continue with this charade, my husband took our seven-year-old out to the car to play with the tablet while I took our three-year-old to grab a stick of pepperoni and then sidle up to the checkout line.

And that is where shit got real.

After I grabbed the stick of pepperoni, I turned the cart around and made a beeline to the closest checkout that had the least number of customers waiting. Lane three only had one person in it so I pointed my cart toward that lane and stepped up my walking speed.

Just as I was about to get the nose end of my cart into the lane, an older lady to my right appeared out of nowhere and was nudging her cart into the same lane. Not being a total social weirdo, I uttered an embarrassed,

"Oh! Pardon me, sorry about that, go ahead." But, as life has a fabulous sense of humor and never misses an opportunity to catch one off guard, my oh-so-articulate three-year-old piped up with this little gem, "Get in your own lane, asshole!"

I died right there. Dead. Gone.

What felt like the world's most awkward moment passed by as slowly as you're imagining it would have. I could feel my face burning hot and tears stinging the corners of my eyes. Embarrassment was turning into shame and I was at a complete loss for words.

To my astonishment, this lady had a marvelous sense of humor. Perhaps sensing my mortification and realizing this was absolutely not the norm for me—and my kid—she let out a howl of laughter.

"Oh my goodness, I am so, so…" I stuttered, looking for the appropriate words that just would not materialize in that awful moment. It was at that moment I wondered if this lady was also a mom because she looked me square in the eye and said,

"Oh, honey, I've been there! Don't you worry about it. He's lucky he's so darn cute!"

I insisted she go in front of me. She was kind to oblige. We all got through the checkout.

A few minutes later I was in the parking lot putting groceries in the truck while my husband buckled our three-year-old into the car. We both stood outside of the car for a moment and he noticed my red face and asked what was up.

"Our verbose little shit just told some lady to 'Get back in your lane, asshole!'" I told him. Despite my super pissed expression, my husband broke out into a fit of laughter loud enough for everyone within a mile to hear.

I wasn't amused. "I'm not sure that is the takeaway I was hoping you would have here, sweetie," I told him.

I guess I was the only one to learn a lesson that day. Watch the swearing in front of kids, for they will bust out those shiny words when you least expect them and are least prepared to deal with them.

Like in checkout lane number three.

*SARAH COTTRELL is a freelance writer living in Maine with her boatbuilding husband and her brood of loud children. She is the voice behind* Housewife Plus *on* Facebook *and the* Bangor Daily News. *Her work appears regularly on* Scary Mommy, Disney's Babble.com, Momtastic *and has been anthologized six times, including in the* New York Times *bestselling series* I Still Just Want to Pee Alone *published by* Throat Punch Media.

# Unplugged and Misunderstood
## By Alessandra Macaluso

There are lots of ways you can screw up as a parent, but I'm pretty sure one of the first things they teach you in all the baby books is "don't leave your newborn home alone." I'm also pretty sure my dad read exactly none of the baby books, because at just six weeks old, that's where I found myself: home alone, in my crib.

Let me back up.

I'm the youngest of six children, all born within an eight-year stretch, which means that by the time they got to me they probably forgot they had me in the first place. My mom had to run an errand that day and after packing up all the other minions was probably like *Well shit, there's no more room for the baby* and told my father she was leaving me behind in the crib.

"Don't leave the house," she instructed—a statement to which he nodded in comprehension and then promptly forgot about, as he grabbed his keys and headed out the door. This was 1982, so it's not like he was distracted while playing Candy Crush or anything—it just slipped his mind. He wasn't thinking.

As an adult I frequently ask my mom what *she* was thinking having all of us kids, and her answer is always the same: "I wasn't!" I suppose I'm glad for her ~~sideshow aspirations~~ thoughtlessness, because it's the reason I sit here today telling you this story (or at least that's the way I rationalize my existence). But my point is, there is something to be said as a parent for thinking just a little bit *less*.

Many of our parents were not overthinkers when it came to this parenting gig. They were far more laid back, and because there were no cell phones or Internet, they were also blissfully unplugged.

And thank sweet baby Jesus they *didn't* have smartphones. I see my dad walking around our house now with his phone in hand, bumping into shit, and I immediately start sweating and wondering if we baby-proofed enough. (Is senior-proofing a thing? Because I think there's an untapped market.)

And because of my dad's thick immigrant accent, even Siri can't help him:

DAD: "Tell-a my daughterrrr to send-a me a picture of-a da baby."

SIRI: You'd like a pitcher of iced tea. Is that right?

DAD: "A PIC-A-TURRRE OF-A DA- BA-BY"

SIRI: I'm sorry, I didn't catch that.

DAD: "A PIC-A-TURE"

SIRI: <SENDS PHOTO OF PIKACHU>

DAD: <HOLDS PHONE OUT, ADJUSTS GLASSES> "Hey! Look-a how cute he get!"

Could you imagine if our parents' generation had smartphones while raising kids? With *their* parents pressuring them to chronicle every turd the baby produced via a "Mima-friendly" app? It's all too much to manage and it's no wonder lots of us are wound up tight, running around like squirrels on steroids.

It's not that my parents weren't strict, or that they were negligent. They just kind of let shit happen a little bit. An attitude which, sure, resulted in some unfavorable things. Like when my brothers would sneak into my room and jar me awake at eleven o'clock at night, yelling at me to hurry up because I was late for school. "Already?" I'd grumble as I'd shuffle over to my closet, them laughing their preteen asses off the whole time.

Or the time I closed my dresser drawer and a giant ceramic sculpture of Dino from the Flintstones catapulted from the hutch above it, knocking me out cold. Two of my brothers found me rolling around on the floor bleeding from my head, and instead of calling my parents they spent the next twenty minutes contemplating whether I was faking it and if the blood on my head was actually Jell-O. And let's not talk about why my mother thought it was a good idea to put a toddler-assaulting dinosaur atop my bedroom furniture, but my guess is the same: she wasn't thinking too much about it.

They never meddled much but when they did get involved, they nudged us to hone our intuition. I will never forget the day I came home from my first "real" job, the one my parents were so proud of me to get, the one that was coveted by many others—and also the one making me ugly-cry on my bedroom floor. That particular day was the last straw, when my boss brought me into a conference room full of all the top executives and berated me for something that was her mistake. I tried to hide from my dad while choking back tears, because I didn't want to disappoint him or hear a lecture, but he found me. And once he did, he cleared his throat, looked me square in the eyes, and said: "You go back-a there tomorrow." My face fell. My father was big on respect and sticking things out. "And you tell all of-a those people to go scratch-a their asses."

Make sure your kids know when to stick it out, and when to tell someone to go "scratch-a their ass."

Our parents didn't have apps and notifications and streaming news and thirty-four fucking parenting gurus in their face all day assaulting their eyes and ears, telling them they're doing it all wrong and the apocalypse is coming and did you pick up your dry cleaning?

Without all these reminders and mental clutter our parents were actually still able to convey to us the important stuff—that "no means no," that if you touch that stove you're going to get burned, that Santa is always watching and for shit's sake nobody needs to perform months of elf-capades to prove it— and let us figure out the rest.

We think so much we now have meditation apps that teach us specifically *not* to think. There are stressors all around us and cutting back on even a few of them can make a huge difference and tone down the intensity of being a parent. I recently removed the Facebook app from my phone and you'd think I ran off to an ashram and drank kombucha with Buddha with the mental space it's given me.

But if I had to convey one solid piece of parenting advice, whether you're a first-timer with a newborn or parenting a clan of all ages, it's this: do less and think less.

While this might sound like an easy task, it's actually a tricky motherfucker to navigate, because in order to do less and think less you have to put in some elbow grease. Our parents, while superheroes in some ways, weren't any better than we are about this—they just had less distractions. You and I have to curate the shit out of our lives and that takes some serious grit. Our job is harder, and that's because we have way more information to weed through than any generation before us in order to cocoon ourselves with the people and things that truly matter.

So, don't be so hard on yourself. Let go a little bit, and don't think so much. Give your kids the opportunity to stick up for themselves. Leave your infant home alone sometimes, because—you know what, no. That one is still never okay. GODDAMMIT, DAD, DO YOU HEAR ME? It's never okay.

*ALESSANDRA MACALUSO is author of* What a Good Eater! *and* The Real-Deal Bridal Bible, *host of the* Real-Deal Brides *podcast, and blogger at AlessandraMacaluso.com. Alessandra's work is featured in several anthologies, and she contributes to* The Huffington Post, Scary Mommy, *and many other online publications. Her original screenplay* Polar Suburbia *placed as a semifinalist in the Moondance Film Festival.*

*Alessandra is mom to two toddlers and a twenty-five-pound Maine coon cat who believes he is a dog. She specializes in driving her OCD husband completely nuts with her constant rearrangement of scenery in their home. Learn more at AlessandraMacaluso.com.*

# Teenage Wasteland
## By Samara Rose

I picked up a pamphlet at my son's middle school entitled "How to Deal With Violence, Depression and Drugs While Raising Your Teenager."

Surprisingly, this was not for the PARENTS. In fact, this was directed toward the teenagers. I'm not sure what they're so violently depressed about, since they spend all their free time in group chats named "We Smell Like Pekpeks," but let's explore how to better cope with our teenagers.

### Understanding the Teen Years

When does all the madness start? There are certainly visible signs of impending puberty, but many kids announce the onset of adolescence with a dramatic change in behavior. No, you're not having a stroke—your kid did just mutter "fuck you" under his breath. The toddler who used to blissfully watch *Peppa Pig* is now watching YouTube videos on how to make cyanide from apple seeds to see if he can get away with murdering you in your sleep.

### Butting Heads

One of the common tropes of adolescence is the rebellious teen continually at odds with his parents. It's natural for teens to start pulling away from their parents, which often reads as a contentious relationship with mom and dad.

You may need to look closely at how much room you give your teen to be an individual and ask yourself questions such as: "Do I listen to my child?" and "Do I allow my teen's opinions and tastes to differ from my own?" If you answered "Yes," thanks a lot! You're ruining it for the rest of us, you hippie loser! Why don't you just move to Portland and smoke the ganja with your kid all day so they can grow up to be a sustainability consultant, WHATEVER THAT IS.

## Talk to Kids Early and Often

Answer the early questions kids have about bodies, such as what masturbation is, and where babies come from. Don't wait until your daughter is giving birth at the prom to talk to her about safe sex.

Share memories of your own adolescence. There's nothing like knowing that mom or dad also got in trouble for having marijuana even though it wasn't mine, I was just holding it for a friend, I SWEAR!

This is a good time to ask your teen your own questions such as:

*Are you noticing any changes in your body?* Well, I certainly have! When you got into my car after basketball my eyes watered and I thought a skunk sharted on my dashboard. How about taking a shower at least twice a week, using soap, okay?

*Are you having any strange feelings?* You are? Close the door and for God's sake don't hand me that crunchy towel to wash; you can prop a door open with that thing.

*Are you sad sometimes and don't know why?* WELL, JOIN THE FUCKING CLUB.

## Pick Your Battles

If teenagers want to dye their hair, paint their fingernails black, or wear funky clothes, think twice before you object. It's not YOUR business if your daughter wants to dress like a Craigslist hooker who drank too much tequila and passed out in the sun. Is she working as a phone sex operator? Drug mule? If the answer to both these questions is "no," you're doing something right.

## Inform Your Teen—and Stay Informed Yourself

The teen years often are a time of experimentation, and sometimes that experimentation includes risky behaviors. Don't avoid the subjects of drug, alcohol, or tobacco use. Just remember, when it comes to your *own* use of these things, LIE YOUR ASS OFF! And get to know your child's friends. That kid with the gauges in his ears so enormous his earlobes look like Betty White's labia? He may not cook meth, but he definitely knows a guy who does. FYI, he's probably not on the honor roll.

## Know the Warning Signs

A certain amount of change is to be expected during the teen years. However, some drastic behaviors are warning signs, and you need to be able to understand the subtext of these behaviors:

- Extreme weight gain—they're smoking weed and have the munchies.
- Sleep problems—excessive masturbation.
- Intense irritability—they've contracted a venereal disease.
- Skipping school often—they finally realized how worthless school is.
- Falling grades—see above.

## Give Teens a Game Plan

Help them figure out how to handle a potentially unsafe situation. If the person who drove them to the party is now drunk, tell them to sleep where they are. Alternatively, advise them to find a ride with someone who has snorted meth instead. Better to have a driver who's hyperaware and twitching uncontrollably than someone who's going to pass out in the driver's seat.

## Respect Kids' Privacy...

In that, they shouldn't HAVE ANY. Go through your teen's room, texts, emails, and social media like Inspector Gadget! Think back to the crap you were pulling at that age. Of course, they'll just find new and more inventive ways to hide contraband, so be prepared to up your snooping game. And you'll have to get used to finding things like Scooby-Doo porn, which RUH ROH! cannot be unseen.

## Recognize Your Teen's Need for Space

Of course, they want space, they feel entitled to the whole goddamn galaxy. Just don't GIVE them any. One minute it's all "free to be you and me," the next minute they're snorting blow off some hooker's ass.

## Let Kids Feel Guilty

Guilt works WONDERS on teenagers, correcting everything from acne to unwanted pregnancies. The next time you catch your son masturbating to anime porn, make sure you let him know how much he let you down. Good luck to him not thinking about you and your quiet disappointment the next time he greases up for a good bone flailing.

## Be a Role Model

In other words, subscribe fully to the *"Liar liar pants on fire"* style of parenting. If you aspire to raise teenagers to be semi-productive members of society, this is no time for *honesty*.

If you have a teenager you're going to have to learn to roll with the punches. You have two choices—you can either laugh when you realize you're retroactively paying for everything you did to your parents when you were a teenager—or you can keep your kid in a medical coma until he turns twenty.

*You know that aging rocker chick you saw at Target? That's Samara, who dresses like a teenager in a frantic attempt to beat back death. SAMARA ROSE is a freelance writer who has been published on* Cosmopolitan, Marie Claire, Redbook, Good Housekeeping, *and* Woman's Day, *among others. She keeps it real at her no-holds-barred award-winning blog* A Buick in the Land of Lexus.

*A native New Yorker, Samara currently resides in New Jersey with her son, Little Dude, the coolest thirteen-year-old kid on the planet. She was told she had the right to remain silent—but she declined.*

# The Theory of Relativity
## By Elly Lonon

There are four things in this life I simply cannot abide: tight spaces, the smell of vomit, ballads performed by Rod Stewart, and people with complete disregard for how they impact this world. Of these, it's the last one that's most likely to send me into cardiac arrest. Only the last one incites anger within me. In our house, we have one overarching rule—you leave places/things/the world better than you found them. It shapes every lesson I try to impart to my children. If you read two books at the library, you put away three. If you see an empty soda bottle in the park, you put it in your bag until you find a recycling bin. If your sweating pint leaves a wet circle on your coaster, you flip it over before walking away from the bar.

My kids haven't quite mastered that last one yet, but genetically the odds are in their favor.

Speaking of my cherubic progeny, they seem to delight in finding ways to force my least favorite experiences upon me. We are fortunate enough to live in a place with fourteen parks within a one-mile walk from our home. There are open fields, baseball diamonds, corkscrew slides, tire swings, merry-go-rounds, monkey bars, xylophone climbing equipment, spinning mushrooms…every possible outdoor delight one could imagine. Yet when they were tiny, my children, without fail, requested to visit what they call Tube Park.

Were they drawn to the wishing tree there bedecked with sparkling charms and the hopes of our neighbors written upon scraps of paper tied to its branches? Nope. Was it the allure of the pristine paved half-mile loop where they could race their bicycles? Of course not. They wanted to crawl through the series of filthy, dark, interlocking tubes (less than three feet in diameter!) that earned the park its nickname.

No, "filthy and dark" still isn't ominous enough. The plastic tube walls are constructed of those same dirty beige curves you see in MRI machines. As though by avoiding white plastic, they could prevent the inevitable bloodstains resulting from organ explosions. Ergo, beige = kid-friendly. At least in the minds of the medical community and serial dismemberers.

Where the tubes meet, there are a handful of what we call pods. As in the vehicles that deliver body snatchers to our unsuspecting planet. I can see no other reason for ever entering such a space.

Each pod has two Plexiglas domes: one is its roof, the other a window. Children delight in crushing their noses against the curves and making ridiculous faces at the parents standing outside. So on any given day, the once clear surfaces are coated in a cocktail of mucus, saliva, and detritus—no doubt harboring a cornucopia of germs. It would be more sanitary to lick any of the waiting room toys at your pediatrician's office than to enter one of these Pods of Plague.

As the weather turned warmer, our trips to Tube Park increased in frequency and duration. We'd load up the stroller with snacks (always sure to remove all the trash we generated—and then some) and the boys would spend entire mornings in those tubes as I perched with my phone or another local mom on a sunny bench. The constrictive, contained, claustrophobic tubes I had abhorred became my happy place. When my children were within their confines, there was no fear of them wandering into oncoming traffic. There was no fear of them wandering anywhere. Nor would they be snatched by child predators unless they were literally snakes. And as an extra bonus, sunburns were an impossibility within their dark interiors.

"We're at Tube Park! Come join us!" became my automatic answer to incoming text messages from the other mom friends I was finally making. It became my automatic answer for everything, really. Under slept? I'll pick up a latte on the way to Tube Park. Under the weather? I can rest while the kids spelunk through Tube Park. Under the delusion that children will tolerate a meal not in nugget form? If the kids just taste the tuna casserole, I'll bribe them with a trip to Tube Park.

Fine. I'll say it. Tube Park became my crutch. As the terrible twos descended on our previously bearable home, I began dragging my protesting children to the park I had once avoided like Rod Stewart's greatest hits.

"We want to stay home and paint!" my oldest, Paul, would whine.

"No! TO THE PARK! It's the only way to snap your brother out of his fit."

In my defense, it always did.

"Can't we just build with Legos?" Paul complained one particular gray morning as I tried to rally the kids for an outing.

"Sam tired," whined the youngest. Not too tired to crush Goldfish crackers with Duplos, I noted. Then he mixed the crumbs with spit, as though trying to manufacture his own grout for betwixt the plastic blocks.

"Not buying it," I mumbled, debating between a mocha or caramel pick-me-up.

"Sam hungry," he responded at a higher pitch, a sure sign we were about to fly off our already rickety rails.

"You can have a yogurt pouch on the way," I answered.

"And an applesauce," Paul bargained.

"Fine," I answered.

"Sam want cheese," the little one added.

"Uh-huh," I answered by rote, throwing supplies into the diaper bag before picking up the little one. His stomach gurgled menacingly. "That's hunger, right?" I asked him, my focus suddenly pinpoint sharp. His answer was a high-pitch whimper. A diaper blowout at the park still sounded more appealing than endless tantrums at home. I grabbed another packet of wipes and a plastic shopping bag before sending them after their shoes.

As always, the toddler settled once the fresh air hit his food-filled cheeks.

After the first block of the journey, the yogurt pouches were flattened. Halfway through the second block, the slurping noises ceased and arms extended from the sides of the stroller, each holding a crumpled applesauce pouch. I distributed the cheese sticks and upped my pace, hoping to make it to the park before all snacks were decimated, knowing I'd need another round of distraction for the trip home.

After parking the stroller, I took a deep breath of crisp air and tipped my head back, enjoying the sun that had finally escaped the clouds. The boys clambered out, tripping on safety bars and the straps of the diaper bag. All moods lifted as they ran to the tube maze and I took a long drag of my iced coffee.

A knock and a muffled giggle pulled my attention to the playground equipment. Paul had climbed into the convex window and clambered for my attention. I smiled and waved, indulging his requisite licking of cloudy plastic. He made a silly face before rolling backward and diving into another tube. I smiled, infected by his contagious joy.

*Yes,* I thought. *Tube Park was exactly the right thing to do today.*

My eyes moved to my youngest in the center of the pod, his blond hair illuminated by the sun so it resembled a halo. He was stooped slightly, bent over against the roof of the pod, his body moving in a rhythmic arc.

*That's such a strange dance,* I thought to myself, moving closer for a better view. And that's when all of the components of the scene came into focus.

The pulsing movement of his body was not, in fact, a child's attempt at doing the Dougie. His tiny body was being racked with muscle convulsions as every ounce of pouch-delivered food erupted from his body. Creamy pink yogurt. Chunky applesauce. *And was that? Yes.* A few resilient Cheerios had still somehow managed to maintain structural integrity.

I braced for the smell to hit my nose and initiate my own involuntary heaving, but I smelled nothing. Because this horror show was taking place within a sealed environment. Inside the beige pod of doom. Only accessible by climbing through dark, dank, beige-colored terror tentacles. That now certainly reeked of dairy-rich vomit.

It was my turn to knock upon the Plexiglas and smush my face against its curves while shouting, "Don't move! I'm coming, baby."

"Who the fuck are you kidding?" I wondered aloud before remembering I was surrounded by other people's children. And, you know, judgy parental types who probably didn't believe in cursing in front of their own children. Or other people's. On second thought, there are five things I simply can't abide.

Meanwhile, I was having a complete crisis of identity because my first three non-abides were in direct conflict with my fourth. But that number four—the one where you leave things nicer than you found them—that's the one upon which I'd based my entire parenting philosophy.

Half of me instantly decided that parenting philosophies were overrated. Just like Rod Stewart. That half began screaming, *Get that juice box and start waving because you need to grab your kids and walk the fuck away. Actually? Parenting in general is overrated. Save yourself.*

The other half was *tssking* and shaking its head in dismay. *You're just going to let someone else's kids roll around in that pile of puke? Let them cake their shoes in hills of hurl? Wait for some toddler to topple over and sit in that sidewalk pizza? Or worse!? And some poor woman is going to have to carry that home! You wouldn't really do that to some poor mother of tiny ones, would you?!?!?*

My shoulders slumped forward, mirroring those of my still-spewing child. Both halves knew I was going in. Mercifully Paul had emerged and was already running toward me. I knelt down close to him and tried to whisper, not wanting to alarm the other parents or draw attention to the fact my child was channeling a yogurt volcano.

"Sweets, your brother is sick inside the pod. Can you go in there and help keep other kids away from the mess?"

Most days, I worry about raising a kid like Paul in Jersey because he is inherently a Goody Two-Shoes. And if we're being brutally honest, a tattletale. It seems inevitable he'll be ostracized as a rat fink by the goodfellas out here. But on that day? I ate it up.

Perhaps "ate it up" isn't the best choice of words in this scenario. Rather, I was very grateful, for he leaped into his role of policeman with vigor. As I retrieved my packets of wet wipes and the plastic shopping bag, I could hear him already directing traffic at an ear-splitting volume, "DON'T COME IN HERE. MY BROTHER IS VOMITING AND IT IS ALL OVER HIS PANTS, HIS SHOES, AND THE FLOOR. THERE IS REALLY A VERY LOT OF VOMIT IN HERE."

So much for subtlety.

I looked back at the tangle of plastic pipes and forced myself to move toward my own personal hell. My knees and resolve weakened with each step toward the ladder. I climbed the first couple of rungs bringing my face level with the tube opening. I was simultaneously hit with the shouts of my oldest child and a wave of spew-scented air. "I DIDN'T KNOW PEOPLE HAD THAT MUCH VOMIT INSIDE," echoed down the tube.

Then I heard the cries of my youngest, spent from the sick. And the soft voice of Paul trying to console him. I remembered my meditative breathing and drew in a sharp breath through my nose. As I recoiled from another wave of stench, I abandoned in-through-the-nose and let my mouth hang open.

"I'm coming, love," I promised. "Mom's coming."

I stretched one arm through the circular opening and then the other, pulling my head into the darkness. Ahead, under the dome of light, I could see Sam leaning against Paul for a hug. "Wait!! You'll get it on…" I called to them, too late. I heard the soft squish of marinated, masticated cheese stick between their chests. Then, as they both turned to look at me, the squelch of their shirts pulling apart.

"YOU WON'T BELIEVE HOW MUCH VOMIT, MOM! DID YOU KNOW PEANUTS FLOAT?"

I cursed my husband for insisting upon having a job that paid our bills and prevented him from being at my beck and call at moments like these. I brought both feet up another rung and slithered in farther. The smell grew in intensity, as did the seizing sensation around my heart. I was close enough to see the tears streaming down the little one's face.

"Oh, baby," I cooed, trying not to look disgusted. "You okay?"

He shook his head in a violent "no" and chunks of Cheerio flew from his chin.

"Okay, Sam. Just be still. Almost there."

I climbed another rung and pushed myself deeper into the tunnel. I was inside the pod! I shifted from side to side, scooting forward, until my arms hung down into the open space. Immediately the boys moved to hug me.

"Stop!" I screamed. Which, of course, startled both of them into crying. "Babies," I pleaded while wincing as their wails ricocheted around the enclosed space, somehow increasing in volume. "Don't walk through the vomit. Just let me clean it up first."

Paul had not misspoken. The volume was impressive. However, the peanuts weren't so much floating as lounging upon little Cheerio catamarans in a sea of spew. Still laying on my stomach, I started pulling wipes from their package and laying them atop the congealing pile. Despite many promises made to multiple deities, the fluids were not magically absorbed. Because when one is trying not to hyperventilate or breathe through their nose, they may momentarily forget that no one has ever marketed butt wipes as "quicker picker uppers."

So, instead, I fashioned tiny vomit plows with the wipes and the curved palms of my hands to shovel the still-warm hurl into the plastic shopping bag. "Have a nice day!" it mocked as its sides swelled with discarded detritus.

"Fuck right off," I retorted. It may or may not have been aloud.

"YOU MISSED A SPOT, MOM. SAM'S VOMIT IS STILL THERE. THERE'S A DARK SPOT ON THE FLOOR."

"Remember what I told that bag to do, kid?" I mumbled.

But he was right, again, of course. While the bodily-fluid-minded designers of this equipment had wisely chosen beige plastic for the walls of their torture device, the floor of the pod was some sort of absorbent foam. Because, obviously, the types of fluids that seep into enclosed, dark, private spaces when left unattended all hours of the night are exactly the types of fluids you want to stick around forever.

I considered what teenage me had done in parks and playground (and directly upon playground equipment) with the occasional musician and a case of stale beer after curfew. Instantly, I felt absolved. It was all relative. All of it. So what if my kid hurled on an absorbent surface? Compared to sex juice, there was no way the fluids my kid had donated to the foam soup were the grossest. If you crossed your eyes, one might argue that his stomach acid may well have killed off a few latent STDs. We had provided a service, goddammit.

"Good enough," I announced to my surprised children. "Paul, you go down the slide. Take the bag with you. Sam, you come to me. I'll pull you out on your back and then we'll clean you up outside."

After another package of wipes, a bottle of hand sanitizer, several deep breaths, and a few dry heaves behind the bushes, I loaded the boys back into the stroller and started the trip home.

That afternoon, as I tossed the bag of ralph-related refuse into the nearest garbage can, I also tossed out my entire parenting philosophy. These days my parenting style is more of a theory—the Theory of Relativity.

*When her oncologist suggested learning a new language to help recover from chemo brain, ELLY LONON chose to learn HTML, which led to the creation of her blog,* BugginWord.com. *Her writing has been featured on* McSweeney's, Babble, Scary Mommy, Your Tango, *and a disappointing number of now defunct sites. Her memoir,* Lymphomania, *will hopefully find a home with a publisher very soon.*

*She really, really hates writing in the third person.*

*She does, however, really like hearing from people—especially people capable of preparing their own meals. Follow her on Twitter* @bugginword *or on Facebook.*

# Seven Parenting Lessons Learned on the Soccer Pitch
## By Eli Pacheco
### *Coach Daddy*

My kid climbed into the backseat of my car right after her soccer match, a 3-3 tie in which she scored all three goals—and let in all three goals as the goalkeeper. Just another Saturday in the Under 8 world of Camdyn Pacheco.

"Sometimes I'm pretty," she was saying, muddy cleats and sweat-smeared head supporting the latter portion of her utterance, "and sometimes I'm dirty."

If ever a phrase ought to be stitched into the stinky shorts of every soccer-playing girl from coast to coast, Camdyn Grace got it exactly right. She's the third of three soccer-playing divas I share a last name with. Who knew when I volunteered to coach her big sister's team all those years ago …

Well, that soccer would simultaneously lift and ruin me for the next twenty-plus years. See, for a soccer dad, there's not a lot of the pretty—but there's plenty of the dirty.

I've learned a thing or two on both sidelines of the soccer pitch, coaching each of my girls, and moving the hell out of the way so that some bloke with an accent and great calves can have his shot at it too. (Soccer moms love the accents and the calves.)

Me, I think they're full of shit, these coaches. But sometimes they have great hair.

I've learned to distrust a soccer-complex restroom exponentially less and less as the tournament weekend rolls on.

I've learned not to make nice too much with the moms on the opposing team, no matter how charming. Her little darling just might be beating your kid's ass—or getting hers handed to her by your heir apparent, in a moment's notice.

I've also learned when you're a U6 player, you don't automatically, on your own, think to poop before a championship game. Sometimes when you're a U6 player, you'll have to go at halftime of a championship game. Or during it.

There are better lessons, more life altering, than that, though. Those apply to life in general. Some lessons are exclusively the beautiful game's. Rec or club, coed or no, on the road, at home, in a tournament, on turf, on grass, indoors and outdoors, soccer will slap you with life lessons like a past-due notice for team dues.

I've whittled it down to seven lessons to live by. You probably won't heed this advice. But you'll remember me when you learn it on your own.

Eighty percent of what you do happens when what you thought would happen didn't.

Follow that?

Even at the highest levels of club soccer, and into the college game, when all those camps with European coaching and trips to Disney soccer complexes start to pay off, there's an unalienable truth that can temper the worst post-loss hangover like no other.

No matter whether the team that just beat you has the next Alex Morgan or just another kid named Morgan, when she gets to the car and strips off her boots, socks, and shin guards, it's going to stink to high heavens. Trust me on this one.

Want to find a new level of hell, saved for telemarketers and people who toss cigarette butts out their car windows? Leave those shin guards and socks in the trunk, in Carolina summer swelter, for a week or so. Parents have lost their eyebrows to such tenable stench.

There are no timeouts.

God, what a life lesson. In other sports, when the wheels come off, a coach can call time-out, toss a chair, yell at a ref, and yank his squad off the field. Not so, in soccer. If your team's losing its shit, all you can do is watch. It's like witnessing a pizza slide right out of a cardboard box.

Or a filet mignon toppling off the grill and onto an anthill, where the family dog's prayers are deliciously answered. It's a hopeless feeling. It teaches us all that life's that way too.

I'll venture off with a resolve in my heart and a lineup of cuss words in my throat, and hope for the best. Kind of like life, and mortgages, and soccer matches.

The other team isn't Satan. But they're from the same neighborhood.

We can SAY we hope both teams just have fun. But without a villain, a soccer match might as well be a square dance in pricey spiky shoes. Yes, they do look like they're 16 for a U10 game. (I swear that goalkeeper drove here. And does that boy have a receding hairline and tattoos??)

Soccer dads on the other side are dipshits; soccer moms with them are crazy witches. Their team DOES practice cheap shots, for the final twenty-five minutes of practice. They'll end up on America's Most Wanted, and will probably win the State Penitentiary Cup in a couple of years.

And that coach? What a maroon. Even with those great calves and accent. Without this sort of role-modeling, how are our own kids supposed to learn to despise other departments at work, or Congress?

While we're into yelling … your kid really digs it too.

At the team, at the coach, at the kid, at teammates and opposing players, and especially to parents on the other sideline. When a kid hears her mother or father bellow with the might of a thousand banshees, it warms her little heart.

"That's my dad," she'll say to the keeper right before a corner kick. Then she'll sneak in the People's Elbow to the kid's solar plexus when the ref ain't looking. Such searing commentary from their lineage reaches a kid like no pregame pep talk ever can do. Coaches do it too.

I heard one girl say to another as they waited to check in, their coach's nearly indecipherable screaming still ringing in their ears, "They yell at us because they care about us." This is also a stellar arrow for a child to carry in his or her quiver of life when the dating age comes.

Always—ALWAYS—wear appropriate underwear.

Oh, please believe me on this one. I coached multiple teams, leading a double (or triple) life, swapping out coaching shirts in the parking lot, cramming a Hardee's sandwich I didn't order but didn't have time to correct on the way over into my refined face.

I sprinted to the sideline as only a forty-something dad with sourdough burger in his teeth can sprint, and joined my daughter's team from my club shindig. (They give you jackets and shorts at that level.) Camdyn, so excited I made it by halftime, leaped onto my back.

She slid down my body as I walked toward the bench to give my team a rousing halftime speech to rally them to victory. As she slid, she clung to my slick club jacket and then right down to my slick club track pants, which fell to my not-so-slick dad-coach ankles.

There, in the open space between fields 4 and 5, I stood, pantsed by my own legacy. I deftly reached down to pull my drawers back up, but the damage was done: Everyone from fields 1 to 5 and maybe even more by satellite imaging, got to see Coach Eli in green silky boxer shorts.

With a little soccer ball pattern all over, and even a miniature goal on my right thigh.

My halftime speech went over like a trunk-trapped shin guard. I'd lost my dignity, my team, and a match, all in less time than it took to destroy that sourdough burger (and less than half as it did to order it). Don't get it crooked, parent coaches and anyone nearby who might double as a fireman's pole …

Underwear counts.

Because sometimes you're pretty, and sometimes you're dirty.


*When he isn't hosting incredible guest bloggers or 6 Words posts with his writing tribe, ELI PACHECO is dad and coach to three girls he writes about on his blog,* Coach Daddy. *He's a reformed sportswriter and staunch left-hander. Follow him on Instagram, Facebook, Google Plus, LinkedIn, and Twitter.*

# Some Assembly Required
## So Follow the Damn Directions
### By Christine Organ

There are people who follow directions, and there are those who take a more, shall we say, flexible approach. I am the latter. It's not that I don't like following instructions or heeding the advice of others. It's not that I'm confident in my own abilities to complete the task without advice. It's simply a combination of busyness and laziness. I'm short on both time and energy, and I just want to get the job done.

Take, for instance, recipes. Most people read the recipe start to finish, make a list of ingredients to buy, and follow the instructions step by step. Me? I skim the list of ingredients and wind up making a cake with evaporated milk instead of condensed milk. Or I stop reading when the recipe tells me to place the casserole in the oven, missing the warning to turn the heat down halfway through the cooking process, and wind up with Cement Casserole with Burned Cheese Topping.

Not only do I fuck up food on a regular basis, I'm so instructions-averse that I misread the directions for submitting essays to the book you currently hold in your hands and wrote on a completely different topic. I get lost because I can't read a map and I tell Siri to shut the fuck up. I've left hair dye on my head for too long and ended up looking more like someone from the Addams family than Cinderella. But nowhere has my inability to read the directions bitten me in the ass more than in my role as a parent.

While children might not come with an instruction manual (as much as we sometimes wish they did), there are plenty of directions to read. Few words are as dreaded as some assembly required, yet they are affixed to every piece of furniture or toy your child will ever own.

When I was six months pregnant with my first child, I went into full nesting mode. My husband, Matt, and I had just moved into a new home— a fixer-upper if there ever was one—and I wanted to turn our rough-and-tumble house into a cozy home ASAP. Matt, of course, took the long view and was a bit more patient than I was. He didn't see the rush to assemble the crib, dresser, and changing table, which, despite their hefty price tags, had arrived in flat boxes.

"We have three months before the baby comes, maybe we can wait until this weekend to put the furniture together?" he suggested.

"This weekend?! But it's only Tuesday! How do you expect me to wait until the weekend?!" I shrieked before stomping out of the room.

Fuck this weekend, I thought. I'm doing this NOW. Who needs him anyway? I am woman, hear me roar. Or rather, I am woman, see me assemble this heavy and cumbersome furniture without adequate tools.

And assemble it I did. Take that, unneurotic husband. Take that, patriarchy. Take that, fine print instructions that require a magnifying glass to read. I'll show you I can do it myself.

Damn, was I proud. That is, until my in-laws came to visit and my mother-in-law gently placed her hand on the front panel of the crib, and, unsecured, it fell open like a drawbridge. Amidst the nervous laughing about how we "might want to get that taken care of before the baby comes,"

I had visions of investigations from Child Protective Services. "Ma'am, how did your baby fall out of the front of the crib?" they'd ask.

"Well, you see, officer, the instructions were just so damn long and I was impatient and who has time to read the directions anyway?!"

Fortunately, my husband resurrected the instructions from the recycling bin and fixed the crib. To his credit, he did it all without a single "I told you so." He can be really annoying like that sometimes.

A year and a half later, our son received one of those giant plastic kitchen sets for Christmas, which came in about 1,439 separate pieces. Instead of spending Christmas Eve cozied up by a roaring fire, my husband and I spent three hours assembling this behemoth of domesticity. Okay, so we don't even have a fireplace to sit in front of, but still. Talk about a holiday buzzkill.

Making this chore even more difficult were the impossible-to-read instructions. And by "impossible to read," I mean impossible for me to read, because I didn't read them. Instead, I did a half-ass job of skimming the directions in the hopes we could get to bed before Santa came down the chimney we didn't have. Halfway through the project, we realized one of us (okay, it was me, all right?) had assembled half the kitchen backward. Several f-bombs and maybe even a few tears later, we were back in business and even finished before Christmas morning.

I wish I could say I've learned my lesson over the years, but bad habits fall hard. I've put together entire Lego creations only to realize at the end I put the wing to the X-Wing Fighter on backward, or the doors are all upside down. I've returned expensive toys simply because the instructions are too hard to read. (Drone from Christmas 2016, I'm looking at you.) We've shown up to the wrong baseball field thinking we were early, only to realize the rest of the team was warming up for the game at the baseball field on the other side of town—which I would have known if I had read the email with game time and location instructions.

Then there was the time that my inability—or rather my unwillingness—to read the directions resulted not just in a few extra minutes or hours putting together a toy or piece of furniture, but a daylong school field trip, replete with a long, hot, and sweaty bus ride with forty loud third-graders.

*How in the world did this happen?* you ask. Well, let me tell you in the hopes the same fate doesn't befall you. Like most families, my kids come home from school each day with reams of paper—homework that I'll nag them to finish, craft projects I'll inconspicuously throw in the trash, paperwork, paperwork, and more paperwork.

It was in the midst of sorting through these mountains of paper that I saw the field trip form. I skimmed it for date and location, signed it, and shoved it back in my son's backpack, patting myself on the back for actually getting the form signed and returned on time.

"Can you chaperone the field trip?" my son pleaded. "Puh-leeeaase!"

"I'm sorry, buddy," I said. "I have to work that day… But at least I signed the form on time, right? That's pretty good! Don't forget to return it tomorrow, okay?"

"Okay."

I was damn pleased with myself for being a responsible parent until a few days later, when I received an email from my son's teacher asking me to sign and return the field trip permission slip. Huh?! I thought. I turned that in already. Nonetheless, assuming my son had forgotten to return the form, I signed the second form his teacher sent home that night, wondering why it looked slightly different from the first form. I didn't think much about it, however, until the next day when an email from the teacher announced the field trip volunteers.

"Thanks to all the parents who offered to chaperone the field trip," the email began. "Since there were more volunteers than needed, we drew names this morning." God bless those parents, I thought. Better you than me.

The email went on to list the three chaperones "lucky" enough to be selected from the Field Trip From Hell lottery. I skimmed the list and literally gasped when I saw my name. What?! How could this be? I hadn't even signed up to chaperone!

"Did you sign me up to chaperone your field trip?" I asked my son that night.

"Well, umm…" he stammered. I glared at him.

"Will you do it?" he asked hopefully.

"I suppose," I sighed. "But you shouldn't have signed me up without telling me."

"I didn't," he said. "I just turned in the forms and then when they called your name as a chaperone I was surprised because I knew you had to work, but I didn't say anything because I really want you to chaperone."

And then it all made sense. I had signed the wrong freaking form! I hadn't read the instructions and the first form I signed was the volunteer form. No! And now I couldn't back out because my son was so freaking happy I was coming and I was too embarrassed to admit my mistake to his teacher. Shit! And now I would need to rearrange my work schedule and find childcare for my younger son and…Fuck!

I panicked for a few seconds, but then I looked at my son. He was so damn happy, so I couldn't stay crabby for long. In the words of Bob Ross, maybe it was just a "happy accident." It would be good to take a break from work for a day, and I might as well take advantage of the fact my son still wants me to be around him and his friends. The days are numbered before he starts rolling his eyes at me and pretending he doesn't know me when we're out in public together.

These "some assembly required" mistakes all turned out all right…in the end. But, parents, heed my advice: Read the damn directions. Lest you want to spend hours assembling and then reassembling your kids' toys. Lest you want to build a death trap for your baby. Lest you want to spend hours on a hot and sweaty bus without air-conditioning listening to giggly third-grade girls flirt with awkward tween boys as the bus stalls in Chicago rush-hour traffic.

*CHRISTINE ORGAN is a writer whose propensity for swearing matches her inability to read directions. When she isn't fixing problems of her own creation, you can find her on her computer or sneak-eating cookie dough in the bathroom. She is a staff writer for* Scary Mommy *and her work has also appeared in* The New York Times, The Washington Post, *and* Babble, *among others. She is the author of* Open Boxes: the gifts of living a full and connected life, *co-author of* Daring to See More, *co-editor of* Here in the Middle: Stories of Love, Loss, and Connection From the Ones Sandwiched In Between, *and a contributor to* I Just Want to Be Perfect. *You can find her wasting time on Facebook, Twitter, and Instagram.*

# Never Turn Left
## By Jeff Vrabel

In my mother's world, every morning presented my brother and me with new and innovative ways to die.

Through her eyes, the world was simply full of the outside, a place full of mosquitoes and flu viruses and strangers and deep water and allergen-rich snacks. There was danger in all of it. There was danger in the snakes in our yard, the wasp's nests under the gutter, the sneezy friends, the solar eclipse. There was danger in going swimming without waiting an hour after eating, which apparently triggered an unstoppable physical reaction in which my insides would liquefy into strawberry Jell-O, leak out of my ears, and result in both a gelatinous expiration and a pretty grody cleanup job for the janitors at the condo. There was danger in sticking my hand out the car window, because one of Mom's third-grade classmates once did that on the bus and got his arm sliced clean off. There was danger in the deep end of the pool, which I was encouraged to avoid; I remember a third-grade birthday party at Chris Kirkpatrick's house, watching the other guys jumping in and wondering if I'd ever join the magical Land of the Treading. (Do not even get me started on the diving board.)

It went on like this. Distant peals of thunder drove us indoors, a forecast of freezing rain could spot-cancel an entire trip to the Camelot Music at the mall, which was super inconvenient on the night I'd finally saved enough money for the "Use Your Illusion" CDs. Mom plotted her routes to avoid turning left through a lane of traffic; one night, she took me to the ER because I thought I had something in my eye. I literally avoided eating bananas for thirty years—three actual decades—because my mom once told me that bananas made her throw up. I never verified this information myself—I wasn't exactly dying to run the Do Bananas

Make Jeff Hurl experiment—but I do know this: I internalized her irrational bananaphobia as a genetic inevitability that would result in me, were I ever to ingest one of nature's healthiest and cheapest snacks, projectile-chorking all over the cafeteria/L train/birthday party. (Epilogue: I eat bananas, like, every day now, because they're good for you and cost nine cents for a bucket of fifty.)

Oh, and the dark. There was also the dark. For reasons I never figured out, we generally left parties, Thanksgivings, and Christmases early, before the sun set. I have no idea the logic behind this, but it never got less disappointing, our family piling into the converted minivan while my cousins kept throwing down on the Commodore 64 in the basement, secure in the knowledge their parents could successfully operate headlights. Today, of course, I know Mom was simply trying to escape the exhausting, emotion-sapping clustertruck of a family Christmas, but at the time I was like, I'm just spitballing ideas here, but maybe we stick around an extra hour and Dad could drive?

You read a lot about helicopter parents, and we could kill a solid weekend debating the merits of that approach, but I'm here to tell you being governed by it sucks. At the time, I didn't realize it was happening, of course, but when you're a child you implicitly accept your surroundings as normalized bordering on dull. I'm sure there are children of circus performers who look at the rest of us like, "Look at these schmoes with their 'helmets.'"

But over time, I quietly and sneakily evolved into what society and the kids in my gym class called "a wimp," or "neeeeeeeeerd," or whatever sound they were making when they were chucking dodgeballs at my face. I'd become an overly cautious, oft-unimaginative, unchallenged buttercup who ended up not being pushed into very much at all. I was allowed to quit cross-country because it was hard (turned out to run long distances you needed to *practice* running long distances, do you have ANY idea how thirsty that makes you?). I was let out of track and Babe Ruth baseball tryouts because I sucked. Although, to be fair, I sucked in innovative new ways. Her lessons and advice weren't direct—she never sat us down and said, "Now here's a list of everything that lives in the crawlspace"—but the cumulative effect weighed, and the ending was always the same: Someone will get you out of this. I didn't invent this approach but I became exceedingly complicit in it; I enjoyed the benefits of my vulnerable status when I needed to, and I'm sure my mom enjoyed proffering them. And this went on for two or three or ten years until one night when my post-college girlfriend suggested going out for Indian food and, judging by the look on her face, was not expecting the sound I made, which was something like, "Blurphgh," with an eye-roll. She'd pitched something she'd done a million times with cooler guys; I'm there thinking *but Indian food doesn't include cheeseburgers, what are you even talking about?* And it occurred to me: Hmm, it would seem that there are parts of the world that I have missed.

It likely goes without saying that we've avoided my mom's advice and approach with our own children, and by "avoided" I mean "made a wild, hilarious overcorrection to it." Before I go on, let me assure you that, though we live in Indiana, this does not mean we let our thirteen- and five-year-old play with unsupervised shotguns (we sold them for Mellencamp tickets), roam the cornfields unmonitored (that's where the aliens grab you) or drive the tractors around (real talk though, it's super fun). There are two "worst" things on the Internet: self-help memes with scripty fonts and sunset backgrounds, and sleepy, obvious blog-snoozes about how Everything Was Better When I Was a Kid. Well, and *Gawker*. Oh, and those videos where people narrate themselves playing Minecraft dear holy God it's like listening to someone scrape a stainless-steel refrigerator with a knife and fork.

Rather, it's a compromise, the sense that my wife and I find ourselves erring on the far side, the deep-end side, the eat-a-banana side, the jump-in-the-ocean-most-of-the-animals-there-probably-won't-kill-you side, and I don't know how to gauge these things, but the kids seem to be alive. My son is way more adventurous than I ever was; he's so much less afraid to try things, to meet people, and to get something over with early that I no longer believe in the science of genetics. Being hilarious, he makes fun of my fear of heights ("What's wrong, Dad?" he cackles, leaning over a railing at Yosemite while my palms lather themselves up with sweat) and spiders (he likes to relocate them outside, rather than follow my policy, which is to smush them with a shoe and then smush the smushed parts again to send a message to its friends) and clowns (duh) and whales (the scene in *Finding Nemo* is basically a waking nightmare) and wow, I have a lot of problems as a father figure. But he's more likely to leap, to try. At forty-one, there's still that blip before I get in the water, that pause to look back and see if Mom is motioning me away from the rope separating the Shallow from the Deep.

She did that, of course, because she spent a lifetime carrying all these worries for us while keeping none for herself. Hours before she died two Christmases ago, the ICU doc asked me about her medical history, and I looked him right in the eye and reported that I had absolutely no idea. To this day, I know more about Mom's favorite Jimmy Buffett songs and obnoxious backyard neighbors than her medical history. To the best of my knowledge, Mom hadn't been inside a medical building since giving birth to my brother in 1978. She was deathly afraid of doctors, anxious about something so simple as a routine physical, owing, I imagine, to her two-pack-a-day habit. Mom smoked Tareytons, which you have never heard of, but were like regular cigarettes except with 7,000 percent more tar. And I think she never went because of what she knew she'd hear, what she'd have been right about. Whatever overprotective sirens fired off in her head, they only applied to others. Hours spent panicking about daylight and bananas and swimming after eating, while drawing in chemicals that everyone knows kills you.

Anyway, if there's an upside, it's that those chemicals helped shape my vague, loose approach to parenting guidelines, which go something like this: tumble, play, fall, hang out alone sometimes, lean over the terrifying railings, roam the cornfields when you can, but stay close to the commonly accepted principles of common sense. So, as best we can, we throw chances at our kids, not to force them into any, but to make them realize the world is there, and accessible, and they can reach it if they so choose. I'm positive this will create fresh new psychological problems that my sons will one day work out on their own children, possibly even turning them into banana-fearing left-turn-avoiding drivers who function solely between the hours of 8 a.m. and 4 p.m. But that's the plain risk implicit in our little advice to them, and something my wife and I talk about a lot, over Indian food.

*JEFF VRABEL's writing has appeared in* GQ, Men's Health, The Washington Post, Success, Indianapolis Monthly, *the official BruceSpringsteen.net,* Vice, Billboard, Time, Modern Bride, The South Magazine, Paste, Playboy, New York Post, *and several angry Neil Diamond comment threads, because wow can those people not take a joke. He lives in Indiana with his wife and two sons. Find him at his cleverly named* blog, Facebook, *and* Twitter.

# The Art of War: Picking Your Parenting Battles
## By Michelle Back
### *Mommy Back Talk*

We're at our parenting best before we have kids. After kids, the shit gets real. There's screaming and chaos and actual, real shit that doesn't belong to you. The second that little bundle is in your arms, you feel two things: love and fear. There's literally no other job as important as being a parent that you can go into with virtually no experience. However, you have instincts and basic reasoning skills that can guide your decisions. You can read books, judge parents who are clearly doing everything wrong, and vow to be the best parent ever by sticking to your exact parenting plan. Once that baby is in your care, though, you realize you have no idea what you're doing and that you were an asshole for all the judgment you silently (or maybe not so silently [double asshole]) doled out before you entered the land of parenthood.

Here's the thing: We're all mostly making it up as we go, but we can all agree that one major parenting goal is to lose your shit as little as possible and not raise assholes. (Incidentally, you'll probably realize at some point your kid is kind of an asshole. That's normal. They aren't that way on purpose. They have no idea how to be somewhat normal humans. That's where you come in.)

Early on, it's imperative to figure out how to give just enough shits to have a good amount of rules so you're not living in a lawless land of ungrateful assholes, but not so many shits that you're basically a parental dictator. You can achieve the appropriate amount of shits by following one simple principle: pick your battles. My mom has been handing out this advice for as long as I can remember. If I were to write her epitaph one day, it would say: "She was a loving woman who always picked her battles. She also liked lemon cake."

Her advice is my guiding light in the abyss of parenthood. There are so many battles that can be waged, but there's not enough manpower to fight all the fights. I repeat this advice like a mantra when I feel like I'm about to lose my shit over something that probably isn't important. My mom probably muttered it under her breath when she was raising my siblings and me. It's up to you to figure out what your battles will be, but choose wisely. For example, I gave a few shits when my four-year-old, Margaret, used a butter knife to start sawing on our brand-new dining room table. Yes, it's just a table, but *oh my God*, why can't we have just one nice thing?! Anyway, picking your battles, it's important.

When Margaret is acting like a cracked-out monkey at a rave on New Year's Eve, I think, "Is there anything worth fighting for?" I'm not admitting defeat. No, I'm acknowledging there are times when it's just not worth giving a shit my daughter is bouncing off the walls and will likely hurt herself a little or maybe a lot. Kids get hurt. I mean, I'm not letting her launch herself off the second-story stair railing to see if she can fly into the foyer. I'm talking about getting hurt like little kids get hurt: in weird and impossible ways. Also, we're at home, where crazy is welcome. We're not out in public, where crazy is frowned upon (but crazy happens there too!). It's also likely Margaret is wearing a bathing suit in the middle of winter while these shenanigans are happening. No battles to be waged here.

When my toddler, Niels, comes out of the pantry holding a box of Cheerios while I'm cooking dinner and proceeds to pour them all over the floor, sit down in the middle of the Cheerios pile, and eat a little Cheerios snack, I shrug and applaud his resourcefulness. I carry on making dinner uninterrupted, and Niels eats floor Cheerios. Is it unsanitary? Probably. But this is a kid who tried to eat dog poop, so floor Cheerios don't seem so bad, do they? No battles here.

When Margaret colors all over her arms with markers, proclaiming she's giving herself tattoos or she has chicken pox or she's simply coloring on herself, let me tell you, unless we're scheduled for a family portrait the next day in which her arms will be showing or there are school pictures, I'm not stopping her. I might give a cursory, "Please don't color on your arms," but my heart isn't in it. The markers will fade and be washed off in the bath, eventually.

When Margaret cuts up her birth certificate. Okay, she was two years old when this happened, but still. Also, I wasn't around to intervene when she did this. I was upstairs doing laundry and she was in my office, unsupervised. Maybe this is a bad example. After the fact, though, clearly there's nothing to battle over. Damage is done. Obviously, Margaret knows how to bust some shit up. We did talk about not using scissors on anything but construction paper, lest you think I'm teetering on raising an ungrateful asshole.

When Niels drinks bath water, I casually say, "Don't drink the bath water. I watched you pee in it." I'm compelled to let him know he's drinking his own super diluted urine, but not concerned enough to stop him or drain the bath water. Urine is sterile, right?

I actually pick very few battles. Brushing teeth, not eating too much sugar, not coloring on things that shouldn't be colored on, not cutting things that shouldn't be cut, not breaking things we don't want broken (including themselves and others), and trying to leave the house somewhat on time are my biggest battles. Other than that, I'm like the Sweden of parenting: neutral and I make awesome meatballs. You might want to pick more battles or you might be blessed with drama-free angel children, but the thing to keep in mind is how much shit you're losing. If you're losing your shit all over the place, retreat. Sign the treaty of giving fewer shits. I have to remind myself of this all the time because I can be quick tempered; I don't tolerate messes very well; and I feel like I'm going to snap when the screaming and whining commence. For me, picking my battles doesn't bring me to a zen-like parenting state. I'm not sure that's even possible. But it does keep me mostly sane. Oh, and I think it helps my relationship with my kids. That too.

I realize now my mom, in the most G-rated way possible, was saying, "It's okay to not give a shit sometimes." There are only so many shits to give in parenting. Don't waste shits on things that don't matter.

*MICHELLE BACK is a mother to two short people who she loves more than her luggage, even though they make her lose her shit occasionally. She also has a husband who folds all the laundry and is the love of her life. Michelle writes the blog* Mommy Back Talk *when she stays up way too late, and hangs out on her* Facebook *page,* Twitter, *and* Instagram *more than she cares to admit. She creates viral memes that are entirely inspired by her kids and life as a mother. Her writing has been featured on* Scary Mommy, *and one of her hilarious essays appeared in* I Still Just Want to Pee Alone, *part of the* New York Times *bestselling series* I Just Want to Pee Alone.

.

# When Your Child Is a Poop Enthusiast
## By Susan Maccarelli
### *Beyond Your Blog*

My daughter was potty trained on day one of trying. Perhaps this had something to do with the fact that she was three years and two months old. This was old enough for me to diagram the urethra for her, have an adult conversation about how this whole bathroom thing works, and still have time left over for her to finish her SAT prep work for the day.

A few months prior, a fellow mother saw me changing a poop diaper and said, "You know, if you started potty training you wouldn't have to deal with that anymore."

Much like my biggest delivery room fear, my biggest potty training fear was the poop.

Perhaps because my daughter had been one of the most difficult babies in the history of the world, the universe smiled and gave us a child who did not have typical poop issues during potty training. Refusing to poop, constipation, only pooping at home? Not a problem for: *The Poop Enthusiast.*

The Poop Enthusiast dropped a load on day one of potty training and never looked back. I was so proud! I rushed in and called my husband to look at the little poop canoe. We sang my daughter's praises and told her how wonderful she was. Little did I know how my daughter's poop enthusiasm would grow immensely in the coming weeks.

In an effort to help with your "evacuation" planning, this handy checklist will help you identify whether your tot shows early signs of being a poop enthusiast.

*Poop Recognition and Commentary:* The Poop Enthusiast calls an audience to inspect each and every poop. Each individual in the household must gather around to see the poop, and comment on qualities such as size, shape, and color. Should toilet paper be blocking the doodie, or should full view be partially obstructed by premature settling in the drain hole, a stick or other disposable item may be required to readjust for full viewing. *Expert Tip: We like to use wooden meat skewers.*

*Flushing Etiquette and Preservation:* The Poop Enthusiast may cry real tears if someone flushes his or her poop prior to all members of the family seeing and commenting on it. *Expert Tip: this may be preempted with a digital photograph should there be a morning poop that needs to be captured for Dad to see when he gets home from work ten hours later. The Poop Enthusiast will need to review and approve photo quality prior to flushing.*

*After-Poop Antics:* The Poop Enthusiast is eager to wipe his or her own bum, though thoroughness may be in question. The Poop Enthusiast often runs from the bathroom undie-less after dropping the kids off, leaving a Hansel and Gretel-style trail of chocolate delights in their eagerness to announce and receive visitors.

*Extreme Celebrations:* When The Poop Enthusiast experiences their first diarrhea, rather than a traumatic event that will set them back months of potty work, The Poop Enthusiast will rejoice. There will be increased requests for commentary, photo preservation, and possibly songs. A triumphant call may be made to announce the soupy mess and request your cleanup assistance. The Poop Enthusiast may almost fall off the commode while craning to see their accomplishment, and gives specific instructions, such as "Bring the biggest wet wipe EVER!"

*Diaper Inspection Protocol:* If you have an infant in the house, The Poop Enthusiast will want to be present for any and all dirty diaper changes. He or she will want to comment on the contents of the crinkle pants, as well as the degree of cleanup required. If your child uses words like "saucy," "dirt bomb," and/or gestures dangerously close while identifying whole chunks of food that can still be identified (blueberries, corn, nuts, or the like), you may very well have a Poop Enthusiast on your hands.

*Down With OPP (Other People's Poop):* Lastly, The Poop Enthusiast will become intensely interested in the poop of all adults in the house. They will make post-op powder room visits if they detect even the slightest hint that you may have done business. They will use their CSI skills (or PSI, as it were) to assess the situation. They will not hesitate to check closely for skid marks in the bowl, identify excess fan usage, and/or use their zero-tolerance odor detection to call you out. Mid-dump drive-bys from The Poop Enthusiast should be anticipated if the bathroom door is left even slightly ajar during an event.

All in all, The Poop Enthusiast uses their powers for good, and you are saved a lot of trouble with potty training. Unfortunately, The Poop Enthusiast is born and not made, so watch closely as your little one approaches solo dump time. I have given you the important signs to watch for. Should your little one show even a slightly higher than average interest in turdology, extreme attention should be paid.

Become The Poop Enthusiast's biggest fan. Embrace their special quality and put it to work should you need yard cleaning for your dog's droppings, assistance with an infant diaper change, or just someone to go get an abandoned toy from the bathroom after your husband has dropped a bomb.

Lastly, DO NOT Google potty training for more than ten minutes before you actually try it with your child. Most articles are meant to scare the living daylights out of you and put you on alert for one of 157 things that will probably never happen with your kid. Each is his or her own little potty snowflake and you never know what you're going to get. Sit back with your wooden meat skewer and wet wipes, and enjoy the ride.

*SUSAN MACCARELLI is the creator of BeyondYourBlog.com, a website that helps writers successfully submit their writing for publishing opportunities beyond their personal blogs. She has interviewed over 100 editors and shares tips and inspiration for getting published with her amazing audience of writers. She has been published on many websites and anthologies, speaks at writing and blogging conferences, and created an online course to help new bloggers get published online. She submits humor stories (like to one you just read) to badass anthologies (like this one) in order to convince her readers she can occasionally submit something and get it published herself.*

# Beware of Killer Tampons
## By Kathryn Leehane
### *Foxy Wine Pocket*

"Did you get it in yet?" my best friend whisper-screamed through the gap in the bathroom stall.

"No. I can't seem to find the hole." My twelve-year-old hands shook, and I dropped a second tampon in the toilet. "Shit."

"Well, that should only happen if you put it in the wrong hole," my feminine-hygiene-product dealer joked.

"I just can't figure out how to get it in." My voice tinged with hysteria.

Her voice was calm; clearly she'd put many a period plug up her hot pocket. "Look, I gave you three. Why don't you just try the last one at home."

That thought terrified me. "Maybe … but my mom will *kill* me if she finds out I'm using tampons."

In fact, from the first day I got my period, my mother insisted I use only sanitary napkins. "You're not ready for the responsibility," she asserted. "Tampons can seriously hurt you if not used correctly."

I imagined a vagina without protective gear getting mangled in a rollerblading accident, but being a generally compliant child, I used the damn pads. Unfortunately, those cotton ponies felt like bulky diapers advertising: "She's on her period. And her mom won't let her use tampons."

For months I walked around like the Stay Puft Marshmallow Man (well, woman) with a load in my pants. Clenching my thighs together anytime I lowered myself into a chair, trying to keep the rag in place. And praying the pad didn't fold over and trap my developing pubes in adhesive. Jerking and twerking while standing up to ensure it didn't come loose. And constantly (but not so discreetly) pushing up my maxi muff while walking to prevent any leaks.

Tampons, on the other hand, promised a new freedom with birds singing and me spinning in a flower-filled field. Though I could hear my mother's stern voice in my head, my desire to not wear a panty saddle was too strong. After my friend gave me my first hit, I used my hard-earned allowance to purchase my very own box of tampons. I snuck them into the house like alcohol or drugs or deadly weapons. My very own sanitary contraband.

Without any maternal guidance, I spread-eagled in front of a mirror and finally got that sucker inside while reassuring my Catholic self I was still a virgin. As an added bonus, I gave myself a better lesson on female genital anatomy than my health classes, teachers, and books combined.

For the duration of my period, I didn't walk—I glided across the floor, performing a female freedom dance. I sat down and stood up repeatedly, giddy with the confidence of a whack-a-mole who would never be hit. No longer needing to grab my crotch to prevent spillage, my days of fear and loathing in Las Vaginas had ended.

Eventually my mom caught on to my deception and delivered her infamous *Tampon Talk of Terror*: "Wash your hands before you handle them. Every time! Replace them every four hours. At minimum! Change them every time you use the toilet. Especially if you have a bowel movement! Be careful of cross-contamination. No germs! If you leave them in too long, you will get toxic shock syndrome, and you will DIE."

I whimpered, "You make them sound like they are murder sticks."

"They can be!" she hissed.

While I risked death for freedom, the anxiety ate away at me. I kept careful inventory and counted out the appropriate number of vagina slims to use each day during my cycle. I set an alarm on my '80s digital watch to alert me when my worry-free four hours had ended. I wrote myself reminders in the bathroom to ensure I didn't decompose overnight.

My mother didn't help ease my stress. She'd pester me every month, asking if I was changing my tampons regularly. Leaving TSS warnings in the bathroom. Tapping on my bedroom door at night to ensure I wasn't sleeping with a cotton mouse.

Despite my careful attention to period hygiene, tampon specters haunted my subconscious. In my nightmares, I would sit down on the toilet to change my tampon, with my mother frothing at the mouth and pounding on the bathroom door, only to realize I had not one but dozens of cotton corks still inside me. Or I'd dream I went to the OB/GYN and instead of a Pap smear, the doctor would spend hours scraping out petrified tampons, turning my insides into a cavernous (but exceptionally clean) flesh bucket.

These nightmares tormented me well into my adult years. I would wake up in the middle of the night, sweating, furiously examining myself to ensure I hadn't forgotten to remove a crotch swab. In the shower, I would perform my own pelvic exam to ensure the baby chute was empty. I matched every empty wrapper to a used product in the trash. I was fastidious about my hooha hygiene; I would not become an after-school special about toxic shock syndrome.

When my own daughter started her menstrual cycle, I didn't want to cause her a lifetime of tampon terror. And I certainly didn't want to sound like my mother. At the same time I worried about her deplorable hygiene habits (because TSS is real!), so after explaining how both pads and tampons work, I suggested she use pads for the first year. I might have also made some obscene hand gestures to sway her away from tampons. She quickly agreed.

Other than a few emergency pad runs at midnight, things generally went well on the period front. At least she never complained about the sanitary napkins. A year later, however, she finally inquired about using the murder sticks. I gave both my consent and my carefully worded warning: "Sure, we can go buy some. But you have to promise to change them every four hours and never leave one in overnight."

She squinted her eyes and cocked her head. "Okay, but why?"

I really want to say I sat down and explained everything to her calmly and rationally. That I didn't pass along my own tampon anxiety. That I didn't become my mother. But that would be a lie.

Pointing my finger at her like a dagger, I replied, "Because they can kill you if leave them in too long."

Thus the *Tampon Talk of Terror* lives on. I hope neither one of us dies.

*KATHRYN LEEHANE loves to tell stories that make you spit out your drink. She pens the humor blog,* Foxy Wine Pocket, *and has contributed to several anthologies and dozens of popular websites, including* McSweeney's, Redbook, Erma Bombeck Writers' Workshop, *and* Scary Mommy. *Follow the shenanigans on* Facebook *and* Instagram.

# Cold Shoulder
## By Brooke Takhar
### *Miss Teen USSR*

When I was nine, my parents got divorced. My mom was suddenly raising two kids pretty much solo while working long hours at a full-time job. It was the '80s, when helicopter parenting hadn't taken off yet, so my younger brother and I were classic latchkey kids. We were allowed to roam the neighborhood, make our way to and from school, make our own snacks, and fight to the death over the last pudding cup.

While my brother sulked, I watched TV inches from the screen until my eyes watered, duped babysitters into giving us instant noodles for dinner, and spent all my birthday money on nickel candy and teen magazines, with their extreme close-ups of mildly pimpled teen idols nestled under bright neon exclamations: "Why Corey Haim Loves Swimming! Find Out In This Issue Of Bop!"

When I look back at pictures of my tween years for #ThrowBackThursday pictures, it is an embarrassment of riches. It's a never-ending parade of the very best discounted '80s mall fashion had to offer: lace gloves, hoop earrings I could have hula-hooped with, banana clips, head-to-toe acid wash, pastel crewneck sweaters with a dickie underneath, and perfectly pegged jeans.

The only crime of fashion *not* displayed is the classic off-the-shoulder-shirt look. The reason is very simple, and also very dumb: my mom said no.

There were very few hard and fast rules at home. We couldn't watch *Married… With Children*, we couldn't lie down while eating fruit, and I was NOT allowed to let my shirt slide down my shoulder OR walk with my hands tucked up into my sleeves.

I was a pretty good kid, mostly trustworthy, and only made my Barbie dolls hump each other occasionally. But something about these weird limitations coaxed some rebellion from deep within my awkward soul.

While Mom was at work we frequently watched *Married... With Children*, flat on our backs, while gnawing on apple slices. Every shirt I wore was immediately stretched off my right shoulder once I was in the safe confines of the classroom.

I *did* abide by the "hands out" rule, because, deep down, I knew it was for my own good.

I was not what you would call a graceful kid. All my friends were in some form of dance class where they got to wear lip gloss and pull their hair into high buns so tight their eyes watered. I had to quit gymnastics when I fell off the balance beam 400 times in the first five minutes of class. I broke my hymen on my bike seat when I lost my balance on a "dangerous" stretch of pavement. (Not dangerous at all.) I tried to jump off a swing set and landed flat on my back, the air knocked out of me so hard I thought I had collapsed both lungs like deflated balloons. Despite my best efforts, I took 100 dodge balls to the face. I sank in the water and was too afraid to attempt a cartwheel. I stubbed my toe on every piece of furniture in our home. It was like my skin didn't fit and I had just taken three shots of tequila—everything about moving my body through life was much harder than it should have been.

My mom knew the next time I tripped over absolutely nothing, if my hands were balled up in my baby blue Esprit sweatshirt sleeves, my face and all my teeth anchored tightly in braces were going to make out with the pavement hard. She knew I needed my hands to brace myself, break the fall, catch myself, steady myself, and live to see thirteen.

I'll be forty this year and despite gaining zero grace over the years, have miraculously never broken a bone. I also don't engage in any dangerous activities like giving breastfeeding advice to moms, adult softball leagues, or shopping at Toys "R" Us before Christmas. I know my limits, and I stay within them.

My sweet six-year-old Stella has unfortunately inherited my ability to trip, flail, and bail at any given time. If I had a dollar for every time I said "be careful" and it didn't do a lick of good, I would be typing this on my gold super-computer in my hot tub on top of a volcano while my crew of scientists works hard at creating a calorie-free cheese spray product. She falls all the time, everywhere, on her knees and butt and head, and I am so lucky my smooches still possess the healing power they do, because we would have otherwise depleted the world's supply of Band-Aids.

Stella spends a lot of time with my mom. (Let's pretend this is because I believe this relationship is so valuable, instead of the truth, which is I need a fucking BREAK.) They chat about and bond over adorable things, like frozen yogurt, Netflix, dolls that have 567 accessories, and more recently, Lincoln's assassination. (Thanks, *Mom*.)

My mom is a much more tolerant and free-wheeling grandparent—there is no such thing as "no." *I* couldn't eat Froot Loops until I was ten, but Stella can get three refills of froyo with sprinkles and marshmallows. (That seems fair, *Mom*.)

So I was surprised when a few months ago, Stella stopped in her tracks and pointed with a tiny accusatory finger at my right hand. "Get your hand out of your pocket, Mom, or you will trip and fall off a cliff, and your brain will bleed on the inside."

I sighed and asked slowly, "Let me guess—did Grandma tell you that?"

Unbeknownst to me, Mom had quietly mastered the art of fear over the years. I was told "hands out" because I might hurt myself. Stella was told "hands out" because there are surprise cliffs everywhere and if you fall off them, you will bleed internally. If you have a child you know the *first* tidbit of information they receive on a topic becomes their *truth*, forever and ever, despite what Wikipedia or their mom might say. (My hands have been very *very* cold this winter.)

Just like every outfit I ever rocked in the '80s is now available to purchase from Forever 21, my mom's rules have careened back into play. This guarantees one thing for certain: next time I send Stella over to see Grandma, she will be rocking a fantastic new shirt *specifically* designed to fall off one shoulder.

Game on, *Mom*.

*BROOKE TAKHAR blogs as* missteenussr.com *and runs so she can eat artisanal ice cream directly from the recyclable glass jar.*

*Online you can read more of her stories at* Blunt Moms, Scary Mommy, Hahas for HooHas, Project Underblog, *and* Coffee + Crumbs.

*In print she has short stories featured in* That's Paris: An Anthology of Life, Love and Sarcasm in the City of Light, Only Trollops Shave Above the Knee: The Crazy, Brilliant, and Unforgettable Lessons We've Learned from Our Mothers, Martinis & Motherhood: Tales of Wonder, Woe & WTF?!, *and* So Glad They Told Me: Women Get Real About Motherhood.

*Currently she's drinking black coffee, sleeping, being the best mom in the world, or farting around on* Facebook *and* Twitter.

# Phantom Limb
## By Serena Dorman
### *Mommy Cusses*

Bedtime with my son was a complete shitshow from birth until he was about three. I left no article about bedtime routines unread, and no sleep method untried. First, I cried it out, then begged it out, negotiated it out, only to end up pulling my hair out. Someone could have told me to bleed a sacrificial lamb during my son's bedtime routine and I would have tried it. I was getting little sleep and had no energy which meant I both looked and felt like a Costco-size bag of dicks on the regular.

In my journey to get my child to sleep, I mastered a variety of room exit strategies. There was what I liked to call Crouching Asshole, where you wait until they aren't looking and then duck to get out of your child's line of sight, which transitioned into the Middle Finger Army Crawl, where you slither away on your stomach, middle fingers of both hands in the salute position in a fucked-up game of Red Light, Green Light at zero-dark-thirty in the morning. Whoever coined the phrase *sleep like a baby* sure wasn't around one often, and they definitely weren't getting carpet burn on their elbows or Legos lodged in their spleen while trying to escape from a tiny dictator.

One day I read about the Gradual Withdrawal or Gradual Retreat method. This method requires you to sit on a chair or on the floor next to your baby's crib, facing away from them, and then gradually moving closer to the door each night until, eventually, you don't have to be in the room at all. A sleep method of trickery? Yes, sir, I was all about it.

So, there I was, sitting crisscross-applesauce in the pitch black of my son's room while he cried out like a pissed-off baby pterodactyl and chucked toys at the back of my head. Another part of this method is that you need to be as boring and minimally interactive as possible. So, I just had to sit there like a total a-hole. I could have sworn the white noise machine was saying, "You're screwed, fuck you, you're screwed…" over and over. I followed the Sanity Withdrawal method to a T…for about ten minutes. Once my son calmed down, I thought *maybe I'll just up the tempo a bit* and scooted an ass cheek forward a half of a centimeter closer to glorious freedom. Huge mistake.

While this method doesn't say so, I'm sure that, like anything child-related, it requires the patience to *not* slam your fists against the carpet and scream, "Satan's dick! WHY!?" or strangle stuffed animals in front of your offspring, but of course I failed once or twice. Or twelve times.

My son's threshold for my BS was the invisible threshold of his door where he turned into a pint-sized Gandalf, banging his bottle against his crib railing as if to say, "You shall not pass!"

For months, I sat against the wall outside my son's bedroom and read or wrote or dicked around on the Internets with my legs stretched out in front of his door, because some part of my anatomy *had* to be visible or my son would pop up in his crib and it was game over.

Now, when it's 1:00 a.m. and your legs and mom ass are numb because you haven't moved in hours, you get a touch desperate. The part of me I usually keep hidden away in the white padded cell of my mind, broke out of her straightjacket and shouted: I'd saw off my own effing legs for just one goddamn night of sleep!

That's when I hatched a morbidly ridiculous plan. If it worked, I was home free. If it didn't, I could possibly scar my child for life. It was a risk I was willing to take. See, sometimes when you're sleep-deprived and your ears are bleeding after your kid's twentieth shitty rendition of "Twinkle, Twinkle, Little Star," you're willing to gamble a portion of your child's mental well-being for some shut-eye.

Every night, I was basically acting like a dummy. In more ways than one. Offering up my gams to Id'n'wanna, the red-eyed god of baby sleep rebellion, so he might smile upon me, granting me an hour of Netflix and "shovel ice cream into my face-hole" time. But what if I used a decoy so I could, I don't know, have my body back?

And that's when I amputated my own legs in front of my son. Thanks for reading!

I kid.

Halloween has always been my favorite holiday, and I'd procured a ton of questionable decorations over the years. Including a pair of bloody legs, severed from the knee down.

As the heads of sanctimommies roll from all corners of the earth in anticipation of what I'm about to say, let me first say this: being a parent requires creativity and improvisation, for you to accept people will often wonder if you are of sound mind, and also for you to be okay with the many bizarre situations you'll inevitably find yourself in, such as smuggling bloodied artificial limbs up the stairs of your house late at night.

After a typically chaotic bedtime routine, resulting in my child being not fucking tired—*again*—I took my usual seat outside of his door. After a little while, I stood up. "Mommy?"

"Mommy just has to use the bathroom really quick, sweetie."

In the bathroom, I excavated my set of severed legs from my basket of lotions and tinctures and makeup I used to spackle on my face to distract men from how batshit crazy I am before going out clubbing. What I wouldn't have given for a night of drunken debauchery without the crushing weight of parental responsibility.

With enough wall space to hide behind, I crouched down and slid the bloody, gangrene feet out onto my stage of lies, one by one. In all honesty, when I compared them to my own, which had a perma-Goldfish-crumb coat on them, they didn't look all too different. Thanks, hardwood floors.

I waited by the wall, frozen. Nothing. No crying, no sippy cup Molotov cocktails. *This couldn't possibly be working, could it? Could it?*

I did a celebratory heavy metal drum solo to Metallica in my head. *Hush little baby, don't say a word. And never mind that noise you heard, it's just Mommy putting dismembered body parts in front of your bed. So I can hide in my closet with a glass of red.*

The next morning was like a scene from *Cinderella*. I woke up of my own accord, ready to sing to a flock of bluebirds as they doused my body in morning dew and mice rolled my yoga pants up my legs and over my stretched-out lower abdomen. *What do you mean the fold-over band on yoga pants isn't bonus Spanx to keep my gut sucked in?*

I was able to keep up this sick ruse until my son was big enough to start climbing out of his crib, at which point I was forced to retire my bloody props and we moved on to the Involuntary Co-~~Wrestling~~Sleeping method.

I'm not the mother I thought I'd be. I've gone to some extreme and pitiful lengths. But I've learned a little bit of family dysfunction is necessary if you don't want to raise a complete asshole. And, also, that there's no "one size fits all" way to go about this parenting business, because sometimes motherhood is a bloody mess.


*SERENA DORMAN is a freelance writer, artist, content creator, and potty-mouthed author of the blog* Mommy Cusses *where she makes fun of herself and gives sanctimommies the middle finger. She is a contributor at* Sammiches and Psych Meds, *and has been featured on Scary* Mommy, HuffPost Parents, Babble, *Buzzfeed,* The Chive, Bored Panda, *and more. Serena resides in the Pacific Northwest where she grew up as a Navy brat and learned how to cuss like a sailor. She has annoyed her husband for ten-plus years, her son for five, and is expecting a daughter who she will undoubtedly annoy soon. You can follow her hot-mess mom malarkey on* Twitter *and* Facebook.

# Promise Me You Won't Ever Go in That Bathroom
## By Kim Forde
### *The Fordeville Diaries*

I couldn't believe what I was hearing. Truly.

We had been warned so many times. Too many times to count, in fact.

And yet, there was my sister, ready to do the unthinkable.

"I can't understand why you didn't time this better," I said to her, somewhere between incredulous and aghast. "Why didn't you think of this before? When we were in the restaurant or that other bar? Why now? You know better!"

Her eyes were slightly downcast, perhaps from the wine we had consumed, or perhaps from the thought of what had to happen next.

My words were direct and scolding.

She looked up at me with a shrug and could only offer meekly, "What else am I supposed to do?"

She was resigned. A woman out of options.

"Fine," I said, my disappointment in her palpable. "Fine. I will come with you. You know I have to."

My thirty-five-year-old sister looked at me and said firmly, "Don't. Tell. Mom."

Her order hung in the air, sharply punctuated and without room for negotiation.

I nodded silently in agreement, and steeled myself mentally for our next steps as we proceeded to do the unimaginable: We headed into the public bathroom in Manhattan's Port Authority Bus Terminal.

I blocked most of it out. But in the minutes that followed, we somehow managed to avoid bodily harm, and a colossal sense of relief washed over us—

a true testament to the words of our mother ringing in our ears, more than two decades later.

* * *

My two sisters and I are all travelers by nature. Between us, we have lived in five countries and visited dozens of others, spanning every continent except Antarctica. We have passports that are loaded with stamps of entry and exit, bits of leftover currencies here and there, and countless stories about our various trips, taken both separately and together. We have ridden trains, buses, cabs, animals, bikes, rickshaws, and any means of transportation available. We have wandered in places where we don't speak a word of the native language and are still pulled to explore new destinations whenever our savings accounts permit.

Between and among these travels, we have collectively logged over thirty years of living in New York City, where we have each seen our share of crazy sights and characters.

We are not a sheltered trio.

But long before we took on our adventures and went out to see what the world had in store for us, our mother had a few words of warning for us.

She was detailed and clear and instilled a deep fear that would never release its grip on us: *"Do not ever use the bathrooms at Port Authority,"* she said. *"Ever."*

As a frame of reference, comedian John Oliver perfectly described the Port Authority Bus Terminal as "the single worst place on Planet Earth…a place where cockroaches run up to people and scream, 'Get me out of here, this place is disgusting!'" It is a truly vile part of New York City. The related warnings from our mother started when we were teenagers, living in a very remote suburb of New Jersey, thick with woods and winding roads. We had no sidewalks or traffic lights. Wild turkeys would sometimes chase us to the school bus stop, bears were not a rarity in our neighborhood, and a copperhead snake took the life of our Yorkshire terrier. This was not city living.

(Yes, I said New Jersey, for those of you summoning up mental images of an endless stretch of toxic wasteland highway, that's Sitcom New Jersey.)

Apart from drinking beer in the woods, there wasn't a hell of a lot for us to do in our small town—until we got our hands on the bus schedule to Manhattan, both forty-five minutes and an entire world away.

Now that I'm a mother myself, I can imagine how uneasy these jaunts into the city made my mom, back before cell phones tracked our every move. And, not to age myself more than my three kids can on any given day, but the Manhattan we know today is not the Manhattan of thirty years ago. Back then, as we people resisting middle age like to say, it had plenty of gritty, if not patently unsafe, neighborhoods.

And so, our mother did what any nervous parent would do: put the absolute fear of God in us by relaying—not once, but countless times—an allegedly true story of what happens to young suburban girls in the Port Authority bathroom.

My sisters and I can tell you without a second of hesitation how the story goes.

*"You can't ever use the bathrooms in Port Authority. Do you know what happens to young girls from the suburbs who go in there? Do you? I'll tell you. There are awful men hiding in there, waiting. When they see young girls come in, they stick a needle in their arm and drug them, so the girls don't know who they are anymore. The men cut the girls' hair and change their appearance, kidnap them, and the girls can never find their way back home. DO YOU UNDERSTAND ME?"*

Holy fucking shit, Mom.

To be clear, there wasn't a lot of guidance on what not to do in the actual streets of Manhattan, but the public restrooms of the bus terminal were basically designated as a certain death zone. Go in, and we may never see you again.

And so began years of very close encounters with urinary tract infections for us, as we held our pee against all biological odds, until after we exited the bus terminal on our many trips to the city.

Now, I can hold off a bathroom stop for an unnaturally long time (we all have our talents). But you add alcohol into the equation and things change.

Temptations arise. Danger beckons. And, of course, the second someone tells you there's nowhere to pee, your body goes into panic mode and your kidneys feel like they might, in fact, shut down momentarily.

But no. NO. My mother's cautionary tale stayed in my head. I would not go in that bathroom. I would not end up with chopped, cheaply frosted hair and renamed as Charleen—being pimped out in the South Bronx, while my parents put my face on milk cartons and my sisters cried about not stopping me from using the ill-fated bathroom, despite the repeated and highly detailed warnings from our mother. What jackass would take such a risk?

As my sisters and I got older, naturally we started asking our mother questions about the Port Authority bathroom story. The days before Google were dark ones, after all.

*Where did she hear this?*

*Was it really true?*

*Should we get her some Xanax?*

*Was she moonlighting as a writer for the ABC after school specials?*

She stood her ground. Yes, of course it was true. It happened. She couldn't recall how many times, or exactly when, but did we really want to be the girls to test the theory? Did we want to be the next victims? How could we even suggest being so foolish?

Nope. We promised to hold our Port Authority pee in perpetuity.

College years came and went, and then our early to mid-twenties—all of which saw us spending even more time in and out of Manhattan. Despite hearing not a single fucking word about the Port Authority bathroom horrors on the news, ever, we had a moral obligation to warn our friends. Because what kind of animal wouldn't? And so, we would gasp in horror as they casually walked toward the restrooms before catching a bus. Dear God, had their own mothers not warned them? Were they not loved?

NOT ON OUR WATCH, FRIENDS. NOT HAPPENING. HOLD IT OR PAY THE DEADLY PRICE.

Our travels out into the world expanded farther. My youngest sister lived in Asia, where people sometimes pee into holes in the ground. My other sister spent some time in a remote cabin in Australia, chopping her own wood and doing godonlyknowswhat in the literal middle of nowhere. At one point, the two of them jumped out of a dinky plane together in South Africa that probably had no professional licensure of any kind to send them hurling toward the Earth. And I spent many a questionable night in youth hostels and on the floors of European train stations, often over-served, all of my possessions secured to my person in a backpack that outweighed me.

We called our mother on pay phones from around the world—and, to her credit, she never held us back.

She must have worried every step of the way. I'm certain of it. Maybe the Port Authority bathroom story was a way for her to engrain a constant awareness of our surroundings into us as our flights took us farther from home. Or maybe she was conditioning us to have bladders of steel. If I'm being honest, both have served me well over the years on a global basis.

As we came and went, New York changed dramatically over time. Neighborhoods that were previously dangerous or even uninhabitable became hip and expensive. The gritty street where my sister had one of her first apartments, complete with forensic tape in the shape of a body on the sidewalk the day we moved her in, has since seen a Whole Foods pop up within walking distance. Because nothing screams overpriced produce like a *Law & Order*-inspired crime scene. And the old place where she lived with the flying roaches over a pawn shop now collects prohibitively expensive rent from hipsters. Somewhere along the way, Brooklyn became the new Manhattan. It was an entirely new urban world order.

And you know what else they cleaned up a bit? Port Authority.

Listen, it's not what I'd call nice by any stretch. It still has indescribable corners of mysterious filth and tons of shady characters calling it home. But now there's a microbrewery, and the food from the little eateries in there slightly overpowers the previous stench of despair. Sometimes.

I'm an old lady now by New York nightlife standards. I don't know where the best-kept secrets are anymore (because they are being kept from me), or where I need to make a reservation for dinner. I'm just a suburban mom wearing sensible shoes who is an occasional visitor to the city I once called home. But when I'm there, I see the younger shadows of myself, arriving on the bus in Port Authority from their parents' houses, eyes wide with the glee of overstimulation and the anticipation of the unexpected.

I'm thrilled for them and even jealous of what is in store for their evening and their youth. I want them to go forth and love the city the way that I did, so that it becomes a part of them forever.

And then the maternal instinct in me just wants to stop them from using that bathroom. Because you just never know.

*KIM FORDE writes about the art of domestic failure on her blog,* The Fordeville Diaries. *A former Manhattan resident, she is now a secret suburban convert at home with three young kids. Kim has appeared in the NYC production of* Listen To Your Mother, *and has written for* The Huffington Post *and* Scary Mommy. *She was twice named a Humor Voice of the Year by BlogHer and, against all odds of writing full sentences when her kids are home, this is her sixth humor anthology. When not busy managing her Starbucks addiction and healthy fear of craft stores, she can often be found on archaeological digs in her own minivan. She may also spend more time on* social media *than she is prepared to admit.*

# Lower Your Expectations
## By Abby Byrd
### *Little Miss Perfect*

Here's what I wish I'd known before I gave birth: Once you pop out that kid, you'd be wise to write off the next five years as "anything goes," and any trip as "potential shitshow."

The key to lowering your stress level? Lower your expectations.

As my four-year-old and I rode the shuttle to Hersheypark, I felt so proud that I'd planned this trip by myself. My husband couldn't get time off work, so I'd taken charge, getting our hotel reservations and park tickets and driving us there. Jack loves carnival rides, so I'd told him the park would be like a huge carnival. I had visions of us frolicking hand in hand, shrieking with joy, our faces covered in chocolate. What a magical day it would be!

Our magical day coincided with the forty-third birthday of the visitor's center, Chocolate World. You'd think Chocolate World would celebrate its birthday with chocolate, but no. Turns out they celebrate with an overly energetic marching band. Brass instruments blared throughout Chocolate World's cavernous reaches, assaulting my ears. Parents of little ones with sensory issues should have been scraping their kids off the high ceiling. Jack, who wasn't fond of loud noises himself, covered his ears and started whimpering. I grabbed his hand and pushed through the crowd, trying to get to a quieter place.

"I'm tired," Jack whined when we were far enough away to hear one another talk. "I just want to go to sleep."

It was 9:30 a.m. If he had slept in the car, we wouldn't have had this problem—but of course, he didn't. He was wide awake the whole time, asking when we were going to get there.

From there on out, the day was as pleasant as a hostage negotiation. I wanted to ride rides; he wanted to go to sleep. Then he wanted to go back and get "that candy in that one store." Then he was thirsty. Then he wanted to "tussle like two cats." Then he wanted to swim. That was all he wanted to do. He swims every weekend with his dad—no matter. I knew he was going off the rails because he started overusing the word "enjoy": *But I just want to* enjoy *swimming, Mama! But I just want to* enjoy *that candy!*

Anything I suggested was met with a fake whine-cry and a scamper behind my legs. *Can you walk up to this sign so we can see how tall you are?* Whine, scamper. *Do you want to have your picture taken with this giant anthropomorphic candy bar?* Whine, scamper. (I call bullshit, because he adores that weird-ass frog Hopper at the Fun Zone.) Everywhere we went we seemed to run into the parading brass band. I wanted to punch every one of the exuberant musicians in the face. During this time, we managed to ride three rides. Jack continued to whine as I mentally calculated the cost of those rides. If it was $140 for the two-day tickets and we rode three rides, that came out to about $46.67 a ride. My bank account wept.

I wasn't too far away from tears myself. Dammit! I had promised myself I would be patient on this trip, as patient as my husband always is. I'd promised myself I wouldn't utter "Jesus Fucking Christ," "Christ on crutches, I can't handle this," or "I am about to lose my fucking mind." (Spoiler alert: I said all those things.)

Jack was still complaining about wanting to go swimming, and I didn't know what to do. On one hand, I was the adult; I'd made these plans, and I didn't want to give in to my four-year-old's whims. On the other, I didn't want to traipse around a hot amusement park all day with a whiny little asshole. So I relented. We'd take the shuttle back to the hotel and swim at their indoor water park. Later, after he'd played and rested, we could return to the park. It wasn't what I'd planned, but it was necessary.

At the hotel's water park, he became a different child. He splashed around joyfully and wriggled through the water like a minnow. We swam for the next three hours. We attempted to walk across the pool on giant floating Reese's cups, slipping and laughing; we careened down super fast water slides again and again; we ran through geysers of water and shot each other with giant spraying pelicans. When I got tired of doing the water slides, I let him go by himself as I watched and sipped a high-calorie peanut butter milkshake garnished with whipped cream and a Reese's cup. We barely argued at all, and I only had to tell him to put his penis away once, which is probably some kind of record.

By the time we'd changed into our clothes and stopped by the arcade for a bit, our room was ready. I had this. Things were turning around, I could feel it.

"Can we go home now?" Jack asked, tugging on my hand. "I want to go to sleep."

"How about we go check in to our room, and then we can take a little nap?"

"Okay," he said agreeably. "And then we can go home?"

"Buddy, Mommy told you we're staying here tonight, so we can go back to the park. Don't you want to go back to the park?"

He considered a moment. "If that obnoxious music is playing, no."

"Honey… that band won't be playing," I half-lied. I didn't know if they would be. I imagined myself lobbing a couple of grenades in their direction.

"Mostly I just want to go home."

I sighed. At this point, we were back in the hotel lobby, where the staff was extremely perky and more giant anthropomorphic candy bars roamed in search of their quarry. I put down our bags and slumped into a cushy chair. I started to cry, for the second time that

day. I was tired of everything being a battle. To be honest, I kind of wanted to go home too.

As Jack curled up on a chair next to mine, I called my husband. "I don't know what to do," I told him. "I need advice." He told me whatever decision I made would be okay, and I wouldn't be a failure if we canceled plans and drove home. I'd been a good mom and done the right things, he said. As we talked, a giant Reese's peanut butter cup eyed me. I willed him not to walk toward us. Apparently my subliminal messages weren't strong enough, because of course that fucking peanut butter cup ambled over our way and approached my son for a hug, whereupon Jack started crying and freaking out. HEY. PEANUT BUTTER CUP. MAYBE YOU CAN SEE THAT I AM ON THE PHONE HERE, AND THAT MY SON AND I ARE BOTH CRYING. SO HOW ABOUT YOU GET OUT OF HERE BEFORE I EAT YOUR STUPID, DELICIOUS FACE. THAT'S RIGHT; I WILL LEAVE HERE LICKING YOUR DELICIOUS, DELICIOUS FACE OFF MY HANDS.

Peanut Butter Cup finally picked up on my "do not fuck with me" vibe and backed away.

Fewer than twenty minutes later, I was in the car slurping a half-melted Hershey bar from its wrapper like a rabid wolverine. I'd gone to the check-in desk and told a very nice young version of Dwight Schrute that my son wasn't feeling well and we were planning to leave, so to please charge my credit card accordingly. Young Dwight had kindly offered to refund everything except the cost of the park tickets and sent us on our way with two Hershey bars. "Can I have mine?" Jack asked from the backseat, as we drove out of the parking lot.

"Not right now," I said. "You ate a whole pack of Jolly Rancher gummies today."

No protest? That was unusual. I turned around. He was passed out asleep already. Shrugging, I opened the second melty Hershey bar and began to lick it off the wrapper with glee. I could see in the rearview mirror that my hair stuck out in all directions after three hours of swimming and that my mouth and nose were covered in chocolate. It looked like I had made good on my threat to eat Peanut Butter Cup's face.

I thought I would cry the whole way home, but I felt strangely happy. First, the two-hour drive was the most peace I'd had all day, and second, I realized that, discounting my expectations for what the trip would be, we'd actually had fun. For the rest of my life, I will remember the look on Jack's face the moment he came whooshing out of the water slide before he gleefully ran around to get on it again. Just *that moment.*

Later, it came out that Jack had been eagerly anticipating the Star Wars General Grievous action figure his father had promised him. Had he given up a day in a child's paradise for a plastic cyborg villain? Maybe. Because kids are like that. Sometimes they like rides, and sometimes they don't. Sometimes they adore people dressed as giant frogs but run screaming from people dressed as giant candy bars.

It's better that, much like on a water slide, you don't try to predict the twists and turns. Just lie back, let go, enjoy the ride. And keep your expectations low.

*ABBY BYRD is a writer, teacher, and poster child for existential angst. Her work has appeared on* The Huffington Post, Scary Mommy, *and other sites. Her blog,* Little Miss Perfect, *is riotous but poorly maintained and has been said to unfairly target clowns. Follow her on* Facebook *and on* Twitter.

# A Baby and an Airplane Will Never Mix
## By Kelcey Kintner
### *The Mama Bird Diaries*

When you first have a baby, you know nothing. Which is why you listen to the roughly 489 people giving you advice. You hang on their every word. You think they are geniuses because they had a baby eight seconds before you. They know more. And you know nothing. So you listen.

I listened to the person who told me to change my newborn every two hours through the night. Every two hours? I don't think my infant even peed that often. My baby was probably staring up at me thinking, "Lady, do you think I could get some sleep around here?"

I was ridiculously stressed after I listened to the deli worker who told me my one-month-old baby would be addicted to the pacifier forever if I didn't get her off that evil thing pronto. Even though I didn't know any middle-aged people who still sucked on pacifiers, I believed him.

And I listened to the person who told me I should give my baby a bottle during takeoff of a flight. That way her ears wouldn't hurt. I should have never listened to that chick.

My daughter Dylan was about two months old when I flew with her for the first time. I packed a carry-on bag the size of Mount Rushmore with everything she would need… bottle, non-bleach diapers, organic diaper cream, natural wipes, her favorite toys, a blanket, the evil pacifier, and whatever the hell else a baby needs (I really can't remember anymore).

I boarded the plane with confidence. I could fly three hours to Atlanta with a baby. The guy next to me seemed pleasant and did not recoil too much when I sat down next to him with an infant. Things were going remarkably well! (Don't ever pat yourself on the back for a remarkable trip until the trip is over and certainly not while you're still on the ground.)

I mostly breastfed but had brought along some formula so I could give my daughter a bottle during takeoff. At that point, I hadn't really mastered the whole "breastfeeding in public when a stranger is two inches from my boobies" thing. That would come later (second kid).

The flight attendant announced we would be taking off momentarily. That's my cue! My baby began slurping down her bottle as I expected to start speeding down the runway any second.

We went nowhere.

She finished the bottle. Oh crap. The bottle was supposed to last until we took off. Now her ears might hurt. I wasn't sure what to do.

Again, an announcement. We were second in line for takeoff. Hmmm... I did have more formula. And I certainly didn't want my baby's ears to hurt. I filled a second bottle with formula. She guzzled it down during our ascent.

Huh. That was a lot of formula for a baby who usually just drinks breast milk. Well, she seemed fine. And she wasn't tugging on her ears!

Just moments later, somewhere around a cruising altitude of 10,000 feet, Dylan threw up all over the passenger next to me. Not a few infant drops of spit up. Full-on vomit from his shoulders to his pants to his shoes.

And absolutely nothing on me. Because she had been facing outward, all sixteen ounces had ended up on her and him.

Oh my God. "I'm so sorry. I'm so sorry. I'm so sorry," I gasped. I rummaged in my diaper bag and desperately began handing him baby wipes. But this guy didn't need all-natural, chemical-free wipes. He needed to be sprayed down with an industrial-strength hose.

He looked shocked. *Was he going to yell at me? Spit on my baby? What was going to happen?*

But he couldn't have been nicer. He was like some sort of angel. He was gracious. He was kind. He was seriously covered from head to toe. And he said he was headed to a business meeting!

We were in the first half hour of a three-hour flight. And boy did he smell. He smelled so badly I wanted to switch seats.

And my baby smelled. Well, no problem. I could change her. Except for one little problem. Despite the fact I had packed her many, many "essentials" for the trip, I had somehow forgotten a change of clothes. WHO FORGETS A CHANGE OF CLOTHES FOR A BABY?!

So I stripped her down to a diaper and that's how we stumbled off the plane three hours later… stinky, exhausted, and naked. Well, I wasn't naked but I wouldn't have cared if I was.

Since that day, I've had a number of unfortunate incidents involving children on planes. I had the kid who refused to pee before we got on the plane and ended up peeing in her seat during takeoff. I had the infant twins who had the stomach flu and threw up in unison into vomit bags. I took a DVD player with three hours of battery power to entertain a kid on a nine-hour flight. Which left six hours for walking up and down the aisles. But nothing has really ever compared to that day when I first flew as a nervous mom with my two-month-old baby.

I learned quite a bit from that experience.

I learned the beauty of showing grace and compassion when somebody has seriously messed up your day. Like going-to-a-business-meeting-covered-in-throw-up messed up.

I learned that no matter what kind of trip you take in life, always pack a change of clothes.

And I learned to stop listening to all the people with their well-meaning advice because every parent is different and every kid is different and if you listen to the wrong advice you might just find yourself sitting next to a man in seat 12B for three hours who smells just awful.


*KELCEY KINTNER, an award-winning journalist and freelance writer, is a fashion critic for* Us Weekly, *created the humor blog* The Mama Bird Diaries, *and has been included in numerous* anthologies. *You can find her on* Facebook *and follow her on Twitter: @mamabirddiaries. She has five spirited children who thankfully don't yet follow her on social media.*

# Yes, I've Had Three Kids. No, I Have No Idea How to Put Together a Birth Plan
## By Katie Bingham-Smith

"Have a birth plan. Write it down."

"Labor doesn't hurt; your body naturally pushes the baby out."

"You will be fine, just do your Lamaze breathing."

"There were no epidurals when I had my six kids and I lived. Gets easier every time."

This is the advice I got from women who gave birth prior because I was the first of my family and friends to have a baby and I simply had no one else to ask (not the best idea on my part). And I believed them.

But like every other first-time mom, I read lots of books on pregnancy and it was comforting to read if your birth plan did not come to fruition, too bad for you, but you will live. Don't get too attached to it and be flexible but make sure to discuss your sacred plan with your doctor or midwife beforehand a few times over because it's kind of hard to do while you are dilating to the size of a bagel.

Yes, easy enough, natural childbirth it is. It almost seems trendy. I can push this baby out the all-natural way, because if these women could do it, for fuck's sake, so can I.

Cue the contractions and I realized everyone who ever blew sunshine up my ass with all this "your body does all the pushing on its own and natural childbirth feels natural and you will be fine" had been pissing lies in my face. I kept waiting to feel the natural part of this clusterfuck, but I never felt it. Unless by "natural" people meant childbirth was supposed to make you feel like you would rather be dead.

Nine weeks after his arrival I was still in shock, I looked around at all the people walking this earth. Why the hell would anyone want to do this again? How could they? I had met some lovely ladies who gave birth around the same time I did, as soon as we got together a few times and I was ready to show them my crazy, I blasted them with questions about their labor, vaginas, and holy fuck, they are never going to do this again, right? They told me point-blank, "You get an epidural, honey. Don't fuck around."

So maybe I could do this again. I dropped the advice so many women gave me about how "babies slip out of your vagina and it really isn't that bad, so buck up." I didn't have anything to prove. Shoot me up with the good stuff. The only thing that made me believe I could give my son a sibling was knowing there would be a lovely serving of lidocaine and fentanyl waiting for me as soon as my belly checked itself into labor and delivery. I would demand it. I would get the drugs. I totally knew what I was doing being all assertive with my plan to get that epidural, and I would tell my doctor each and every time I arrived to each and every appointment, and then I would take the toddler out to lunch for a tuna melt so I could self-soothe and remind myself it would all be okay and I could handle it because dammit, I was getting that epidural.

And so it happened one rainy June day, my water broke while my father was visiting and I shooed him out the door because I was excited to have a pain-free labor where I would lie on the table smiling in full make-up because I would not feel the child blasting out of my cave of wonders and no one would tell me to push toward the ring of fire (why do they say that; where the hell am I going to aim my pushing if not to the ring of fire?).

I strutted in there and said, "I would like to order my epidural now; remember we talked about it at every appointment?" My nurse said she had to ask my doctor after checking me because I was only dilated four centimeters, which isn't that much (hahaha, fuck you). Don't ever tell a woman she is only dilated four centimeters when she is labor, or she just might pee in your face the next time you check her, which I might have done. I can't remember from all the pain I was in from *not* having an epidural.

"Oh, the doctor is fine with it; I have already discussed it with her a zillion times, thankyouverymuch. Please, I want it now."

As luck would have it, my doctor was not available and some other doctor I had never met before marched in wearing slacks and a very stiff button-down with her arms crossed and said, "I am going to hold off on the epidural. I don't like to dole them out so fast, let's wait," then she spun on her heel and left. I had visions of grabbing her by the collar and pulling her in close to tell her I liked doling out my fists into certain faces, so she better give me the goods and give them to me now, but I didn't. Not because I thought it was the right thing to do, but because I was hyperventilating from the pain.

Well, wouldn't you fucking know that a half hour later, I had to push. My ring of fire was blazing and I wasn't hiding my pain. The nurse came in and informed me I probably didn't have to push, I was only four centimeters the last time she checked me a half hour ago, and also, I probably didn't know my body at all.

I bore down and pushed through a long contraction while she stood there watching me, and I can only assume the reason she pulled the tray of supplies over so quickly was because she saw my daughter's head crowning, you know, because I had to fucking push and a mother in labor knows what she is talking about.

So here I was (again), epidural-free, hoarse as well, a mother in labor, and the doctor rushed in just in time to catch my beautiful daughter. My birth plan was in the shitter, but I followed the advice of the stupid books and I didn't freak out (that much), and while I didn't die, I felt I came close. In fact, I think I saw the light once or twice.

When my third child was accidentally planted in my uterus one snowy Valentine's night after too much wine and chocolate, I was sure this would be the time I got to experience childbirth without feeling it because that was the only way this child was going to come out. Besides, what are the chances I wouldn't get to have the epidural again?

I changed doctors, wrote a letter to the hospital about how the last doctor treated me, and explained that could not happen again because everyone else got an epidural and I wanted the experience of not feeling like I was being turned inside out, so please, let me have this.

And as I entered that same delivery room for the third time in three years, and my pain was four on a scale of one to ten (fucking four) I said it loud and clear. "I WILL TAKE MY EPIDURAL NOW!" and I was met with "Oh honey, this is a small hospital and both of our anesthesiologists are in life-saving surgery right now. It is going to be a while. But it's okay, you are only four centimeters dilated. I bet you have a while."

*Don't be a bitch, don't throw things, don't hurt anyone, holy mother of God, no. I am four centimeters dilated, the magic number, that means we have exactly a half hour until I give birth to this beast without drugs. Oh please, what I wouldn't give to smoke a j-bone right now. Maybe I can get a dealer on the phone really quick. Is that how it works? I have no idea; I haven't been high since 1996. Please kill me now.*

Not only were all the anesthesiologists tied up during my entire six-hour labor, the cherry on top was the knock on the door while my child's head was crowning. My epidural had arrived, a bit late, but I invited him in anyway. "Get the hell in here now. Don't listen to the doctor; it is not too late" were my exact words, but alas, it *was* too late.

And after birthing my third child, the nurse measured his head and declared it was the biggest one she had measured in her twenty-nine-year career. Well, fuck me. No wonder I was still craving the lower-body-numb feeling after he was out and lying on my chest. I just gave birth to a watermelon head.

The advice: "You can do it the all-natural way; you will be fine" didn't work out. And the advice: "Just get an epidural, honey" didn't work out for me either. Sometimes life can be a dick like that. And you bet your ass I keep my mouth shut when a pregnant woman asks me for advice regarding her birth plan. It has been over a decade since my youngest was born and I'm still not over it. Clearly I am not the one to ask.

*KATIE BINGHAM-SMITH had three kids in three years and crafts her ass off in order to stay sane. You can often find her wearing faux leather pants, drinking Diet Coke, and paying her kids to rub her feet. She is a staff writer for* Scary Mommy *and regular contributor to* Babble, Mom.me, *and* Grown and Flown. *Feel free to harass her on* Instagram *and* Facebook.

# The Best Way to Deal with a Bully, Ignore Them
## By Mandy Brasher

We ignored a lot of things during my childhood: the strange smell emanating from our food pantry, the spine-tingling sound of little claws scaling the insides of our walls, and the enormous pile of unopened bills my mom strategically hid in the drawer under our rotary phone. Ignoring was in our DNA, it was our family crest. We were also taught to ignore bullies.

"They are just doing it to get a rise out of you, so the best thing you can do is ignore them."

Ignore them, I did. When my next-door neighbor Edna followed me onto the school bus oinking like a pig in order to let everyone know I had a pig nose, I ignored her. She would sit at the front of the bus, right behind our deaf and/or oblivious bus driver, look up in the oversized mirror over the driver's head until she found me watching her, and use her hand to pull her nose up in such an exaggerated manner I could only hope it would stay that way. Or that she would drink a gallon of shellac during woodworking class and die before we met on the bus again in seven hours. Like a good girl, I ignored her.

"She's just jealous of how pretty you are."

Best of intentions, Mom, but unless you had cataracts at age thirty we were both aware of my freakish resemblance to the girl on *The Craft*. The ugly one. My boobs took up half the bench seat on any bus and I had yet to be indoctrinated into the wily world of eyebrow grooming. I regularly cut my own bangs in order to look like the pretty girls in my *Seventeen* magazines. Edna Finklestine wasn't jealous of how pretty I was, she was just a fucking bully.

And she wasn't the only one.

Sweet Margo from my science class took it upon herself to unzip my shirt in front of the entire class one afternoon. Instead of putting her in a chokehold and breaking her wrist, I ran to the bathroom sobbing with my tatas hanging out. The principal's office was just across the hall from that stank bathroom, so I dragged my sopping wet face and 600-pound boulders through his door because ignoring this particular situation didn't seem to be my best option.

The overweight, undersexed principal looked at me with pity, probably due to the caterpillar crawling across my forehead, and gave me yet another piece of adult turd wisdom.

"Kids will be kids."

They certainly will, Freddy Krueger. Guess I better get used to that. That gibberish made me want to roll up his cold body inside the flag hanging above his desk that proudly proclaimed "Home of the Roadrunners."

My mom picked me up early from school that day and after I told her what had happened, she looked over at me from the driver's seat of our prison-style van, her bubbly optimism burning a hole in my blackened heart, and said, "I'm sorry that happened, but you have to really ignore those bullies." So now instead of just ignoring them, I had to "really ignore" them. This stream of consciousness had not been working so well for me thus far in my life. Regardless of my eyes-down, shameful walk down the hallways of my school, or the insanely large T-shirts I wore to cover the fat bags with nipples that hung from my chest, the bullies could smell me like I was an Auntie Anne's pretzel shop in the mall.

The hazing continued at a steady pace and I was beginning to see my future very clearly…it included poles, dollar bills shaped like cocaine straws, and forgotten dreams. My amplified growth in the chesticles department didn't help me with my other nemesis…gym class. There weren't enough sports bras or rolls of duct tape available on the planet to keep me from having black eyes every time we were forced to run laps. And we ran laps every fucking day.

Gym class began with having to undress in front of sixty of my closest bullies. To this day, the only talent I possess is the ability to change out of an entire outfit without having any skin show. We would all shuffle out to the

161

sweat-logged gymnasium for roll call before walking across three hayfields to get to the high school track. The day I gave up on ignoring bullies came to pass on our way back to the showers after another eye-bruising day of jogging.

The mean girls were hazing another classmate and as I walked alone behind them, something inside me was set on fire. It was that feeling you get when you watch a puppy-abuse commercial accompanied by the sweet voice of Sarah McLachlan.

"You better leave her alone." My own voice surprised me and I immediately wanted to die.

"Mind your own business, bitch," the leader warned me. Her glare made my heart race and I was convinced I was going to poop my gym shorts.

I didn't respond to her warning and we all filed into the shower room where I pulled out my magician skills to throw on my Nine Inch Nails T-shirt before taking a quick peek in the floor-to-ceiling mirror at the end of the shower room.

From behind, I was shoved into the mirror. I heard a voice say, "You like retards?"

When I turned around, the bully from outside was standing three inches away from me in all her glory. Dark eyeshadow, long shimmery hair, and a face that asked me the universal question....*You ready to ignore me too?*

I wasn't. I grabbed her luxurious dark hair with my left hand, pushed her down to the tile floor with my right hand, made a fist, and punched her in the nose while I hit her head against the pink tile floor. My ears rang, like the time I dove far too deep in the public pool and couldn't get to the surface before my eardrums popped. The pressure I put on her chest with my knee was exhilarating, and it scared the living shit out of me.

It ended as quickly as it had begun. She looked at me in shock and slunk out of the shower room with her minions in tow while I stood there shaking and waiting for the police to come arrest me. I realized later, that's not how school fights end.

Ignoring bullies works for a while, but sometimes a bitch needs a punch to the nose.

*MANDY BRASHER is a barista by day and humor writer by night, residing in suburban Utah with her two kids and one husband. She frequently offends the Mormon neighbors with her saucy language and apathetic attitude toward undergarments. Mandy entertains her mother on a blog,* mandybrasher.com, *where she rants about gas station predators, being married to an optimist, and her inability to finish writing a book—a memoir projected to be finished post-mortem. Her writing has been featured on* The Good Men Project, *Maria Shriver's blog,* In the Powder Room, *and* Blunt Moms. *Find her on Twitter: @brashermandy. If you like pictures of yoga pants and beer bottles, follow her on Instagram: @mandybrasher.*

# The Cure for Parenthood
## By Jeff Terry
### *Jeff & Jill went up the hill*

Ours is the early-model SUV with Happy Meal stickers all over the inside. Ours is the house with crayon drawings scrawled on the front-room windows—windows that I refer to as "Southside Stained Glass." Ours is the social calendar full of children's parties and early nights. Ours is the medicine cabinet full of tasty remedies in small, chewable doses. Ours are the date nights spent constantly checking text messages and inevitably dominated by conversations about the kids. Ours is a past I can barely remember.

I'm not blaming anyone. I'm a grown-ass man, I can take it. Jill and I did this to ourselves.

We didn't know what we were getting into, of course. We didn't plan on destroying our faces with worry lines. We had ideas about parenthood based on sitcoms and secondhand exposure. But we had no idea that parenthood would suck this bad. At least not our parenthood.

Whenever we bothered to think about it, as we dined luxuriously at our favorite restaurant, spending wads of our vast combined disposable income, we envisioned our parenthood as nothing but love and wisdom. We were certain we would raise our kids with a firm grasp on the human condition and instruct them with all of history's accumulated wisdom.

That's not how it went down. As I would discover, parenting triggers the sympathetic nervous system. It's mostly "fight or flight." Your expectations are worthless.

Since becoming a parent, I've had a lot of time to think about where it all went wrong. It went wrong so damn fast. During those times when I otherwise would have been doing something enjoyable, I've asked myself,

"How did it get like this?" With resentments and frustrations mounting, and the Diaper Champ overflowing, and the gray blanket of weariness smothering the entire world, I'd croak out, "How?"

I'm probably the worst person I could ask because I'm the one who led me here. But in my deliriums, I've actually landed on an answer that satisfies (if you haven't had a lot of sleep and you don't think about it too long). The answer is: It's not my fault. Or your fault. Or anyone's fault. Because parenthood is a contagious disease.

That's right. Again(if you don't think about it) it makes a lot of sense. All of the sense.

Like most viruses, parenthood thrives on human contact. It rides on the current established by countless generations of reproduction.

It's contagious in the most insidious way. It's like smoking. Even though we can witness, firsthand, the devastation caused by parenting, it spreads. Because parents try to hide how miserable they are, and babies can be cute, bubbly creatures in the daylight, parenting might look cool to an outsider. Like something you could try. But there is no try. There is no walking away.

Even when the facts are staring us in the face, we try to ignore them. We tell ourselves it's something other people get. It's something our parents suffered. An old-timey ailment for old people who never had the proper vaccinations. Something that felled careless friends who were smitten and in the early stages of being "in love." Something that strikes down the uneducated.

We witness the struggles that other parents have and we understand, clearly, that their struggles are directly tied to their own missteps. It's obvious. As a parent, we would have seen that shit coming a mile away and not wasted one minute of sleep. And that's not Monday morning quarterbacking at all.

It plays on your narcissism. You see kids and begin wondering what a little you will act like. What accomplishments your little you can achieve with your patient coaching. What you will be like as a parent. How you could undo all the parenting mistakes that your parents made. How many wrongs you and your little you can right. No one's ever parented like you before. You have bottomless patience.

You will parent the shit out of your kids.

In your imagination, your little you does everything you would want them to do. Sure, you might mix it up and "get real" and understand that your little you will need to be disciplined occasionally—you're not so full of yourself that you think you're perfect—but even in your most pragmatic imaginings, sooner or later, your little you comes to see things your way. Because you've properly bonded with them. Because you're enlightened. On a Gwyneth Paltrow level. Or maybe even Oprah.

But don't be fooled, parenthood is sexually transmitted oppression. It doesn't care how enlightened you are, or how much money you make. It waits. Then one day, at the end of the sex rainbow, you find your own pot of puking, shitting tyranny.

As soon as kids squirt out they impose their will, changing the sleeping arrangements and napalming sexy times. And they do it without speaking a word. They force you to guess what their screams mean. You carry the sonic bomb around with you until you stumble upon the way to deactivate it. Sometimes they scream just for the fuck of it. Unbelievably, it only gets worse once they have access to your native language. They become even less compromising.

Over the steady, corrosive drip of years, with bills accumulating and playdates scheduled and Christmases transformed into festivals of lies and pain, I'd whimper, "How did this happen? What did I do to deserve this?"

Because I don't remember ruining my parents' lives. When I was the kid the dynamic was different. I listened and did as I was told with the understanding that if I did things just right I would be given the keys to the kingdom someday. I would be the parent and I would be in charge.

Somewhere along the way, someone revised this contract. Maybe it was my generation. Maybe it was progress. Maybe it was inevitable. At some point the power shifted. Parents became tenderized. And ultimately terrorized.

I remember freedom. The freedom to plummet from a tree and break my fall with my face. The freedom to set up ramps of questionable integrity and jump them on my bike only to inevitably slip off the pedals in midair and slam my balls into the bike frame as I came crashing down. The freedom to test the limits of the law, gravity, and my teenaged liver as I climbed up on garage roofs to drink whiskey I stole from my alcohol-abstaining parents. I remember freedom. Good goddamned American freedom.

I remember the freedom that came with not being reachable. The freedom to walk endless miles in the winter as Chicago sludge numbed my feet despite being protected by the best boots Payless ShoeSource could mark down. The freedom to explore truck yards and construction sites and step around rusty nails in search of discarded treasure. To let the sun be my timepiece. To not compare the life I was living to the lives other people were portraying because social media sites only existed in the minds of Ray Bradbury and sci-fi writers at that time.

I remember such freedoms! And now as an adult, I understand that those were my parents' freedoms too. They threw the door wide and trusted that I had the sense to avoid major disaster or change for the pay phone if I didn't.

It's not that the world was safer back then, it was just quieter. We didn't have 24-hour news crawls reminding us about how dangerous the world could be. We didn't have videos of brawls shared hundreds of thousands of times demonstrating just how out of control the youth has become. Our brawls were school hallway rumors. Our news was on our doorstep in the morning or on our TV at 5:00 p.m. Our misdeeds played out beyond the purview of surveillance cameras and screeching pundits.

We survived without bike helmets and seat belts and trigger warnings. We weren't constantly being told the world is going to eat us.

Now in the age of the Mommy Wars, with the older two beating the hell out of each other over the last scoop of vanilla ice cream and the youngest trying to play in the snow while wearing nothing but shorts, I sip my beer and murmur, "How can I save others?"

I'm the worst person to answer this because I work in marketing. So I produce nothing but thoughts and direct mail. We all know that Twitter has rendered thoughts worthless. And direct mail is killing the planet.

But ideas (without the skills and ambition to build on any of them) are all I've got.

So here's my idea:

We create a series of apps that bring home the reality of parenting. These are all very simple and when you read the descriptions, you might think they're no big deal. That's fine. Because that's the thinking we're trying to cure. Thinking that way leads to terminal parenthood.

The first app is called Noo—pronounced "new" as in newborn—but, deliciously, spelled to capture what you'll be screaming once this app has been on your phone for six months. It'll cause your phone to scream at random intervals throughout the night. And day. It will track your movements and demand to be held and rocked to sleep. It will scream and scream and scream and scream. And then it will scream. It will never lose intensity until you have satisfied a randomized need. Sometimes it will force you to drive it around in your car to stop the screaming. As advancements in tech are made, it's my hope to somehow include an update to Noo that makes your phone spew shit.

The second app, TerribleToo, hijacks your device. If you're talking to someone on your phone (yes, people still do that), a toddler's voice will interrupt your conversation to ask you who you're talking to and if you can take them to the park or make them chicken nuggets. Telling the voice that you can't talk right now won't do jack shit. You will keep getting interrupted for as long as you're on the phone. Sometimes, if you're texting someone, a kid's game will launch and you will lose access to your phone while the game is playing. After a while, the screen will grow foggy, appear to have cracks, and become less and less responsive.

The final app is the least thought out. Because my kids aren't teenagers yet, I'm happy to crowdsource ideas for this one. I call it TeenRager. This app will block you on social media and autocorrect everything you're trying to text and argue with you and tell you that you don't know anything and it can't wait until it has enough money to move out. Then it will ask to be driven to the movie theater. Oh, it will also empty your bank account.

So that's all the hope this marketing professional can offer. I hope someone with actual skill will bring my apps to life. I'm too busy parenting and avoiding parenting to learn how to do it myself. But together, maybe we can raise awareness about what it means to raise children, and blood pressures, and debt, and glass after glass of wine.

Because once you have children, it's terminal. They hijack your heart. You experience love on an entirely new level. And the first time they hand you a drawing they made of you, you will crumble into a pile of every tender emotion you didn't know you had. And then your fate will be sealed.

*Well, here he is, the most forgettable guy on the Internet. And yet, somehow, he made his way to you. Look at that. JEFF TERRY normally blogs at jeffandjillwentupthehill to the adulation of his tens of followers. Now you can say you read him before he became popular. Just don't wait for him to become popular. You can subscribe to his blog, like him on Facebook, or just pity him from afar. He lives in Chicagoland with his wife, three kids, and countless regrets.*

# Oh Shit
## By Julie Burton
### *Bug-Bytes*

*Shit.*

It's just a word. Four letters picked from the alphabet. S-H-I-T. It's in the dictionary. If you look it up, you will find shit is a noun. *I stepped in dog shit.* It is also a verb. *I shit you not.* And it's an exclamation of disgust, anger, or annoyance. *Oh shit!*

Shit is not a new word. It dates back to the Old English *scitte* from the 1500s meaning "purging, diarrhea."

"I don't give a shit" appeared in the 1920s.

The 1930s gave us "Up shit creek."

"Shit-faced drunk" is 1960s slang.

And my personal favorite, "Same shit, different day," is from the late 1980s.

Shit's been around for a long time.

There are times you shouldn't use the word shit because you'll appear, oh, let's just say *disrespectful and unintelligent*—at a job interview, at church, or in the presence of your boyfriend's grandmother.

But there are times when cursing makes complete sense because it's a release. It evokes emotion and it feels good. Cursing is acceptable in places such as at a football game, chatting with a good friend in your own home, and in your car because the car in front of you won't *step on it, you piece of shit.*

Shit is what most parents call a "bad word." Ask any preschooler.

I've been a parent for almost eleven years. I am a mom to two daughters. Emma is ten and Kate is seven. I am not a teacher. I don't know anything about child development. I'm not qualified nor did I study how to raise a child. I say shit when I drop my cell phone. I yell, "Look at that ass!" when my husband walks in the room. It's possible my kids have heard shit along with other 4-letter words flying out of my mouth during a football game.

My daughters know there are certain words adults use to speak to other adults and kids are not allowed to use them. Although, years ago during a park playdate, the only way I could explain to five-year-old Emma the reason the kid whipped it out and peed on her was because he was a product of rude assholes. It was true.

I don't need a child psychologist to tell me kids learn from a parent's behavior.

Yet, I still stared at the road in bewilderment the day Kate mumbled "Oh shit" from the backseat when I slammed the car brakes. I'm trying my best to raise two respectable women in this world. It would not be shocking to me if one day my daughters will be cursing at football games and possibly slipping an f-bomb in front of their boyfriend's grandmother. I just didn't think "Oh shit" would appear at age six in the backseat of my car.

I brought the car to a complete stop. I angled my rearview mirror toward Kate. Kate's blond head was down, looking at her iPod.

*Did she just say, "Oh shit"?*

"Hey, Kate. What'd you say, baby?"

"Nothing, Mommy."

*Oh God, she knows.*

*It's fine. I can handle this. I've heard of kids cursing at a young age. I'll stop saying profanities out loud. Easy. My girls are not little kids anymore. They know damn well what they're saying.*

*Stop. I'll stop. The bad language stops now.*

We arrived home. Emma got out of the car and ran into the house. I stepped out of the car and opened Kate's car door.

"Let's go, princess."

Kate dropped her iPod on the driveway.

"Oh shit," my sweet angel said.

*OH SHIT.*

*Ignore her. Yes, that's what the parenting experts say. If you bring attention to the bad word, your child will keep doing it. I will not laugh or even crack a smile. When Kate realizes she's not getting attention for her choice of words, she'll stop. I'll ignore her.*

It worked. I didn't hear a shit, goddammit, asshole, motherfucker, or go to hell the rest of the evening.

My husband, Scott, came home from work. I told him about the newfound word Kate added to her vocabulary.

"What do you mean you didn't say anything to her?"

"Scott, I know her. If I tell her no, she'll keep doing it behind my back. It was a slip. She hasn't said it since. Or maybe I was just hearing things. Maybe she said shoot and I misheard her. Forget I said anything. We're good."

"You know she gets this from you."

"Um, no, jackass. She doesn't. That would be your daughter. You cuss in front of the TV all the time."

"You need to say something to her. Ignoring her won't solve the problem."

"All the parenting experts say don't bring attention to it."

"Yeah, for a two-year-old! She's six! She knows what she's saying. Tell her to come here."

"No. It's too late. Talk to her if she says it again. It's really not that big of a deal."

"Do you want her sounding like complete trash?"

"Are you saying I'm trash?"

A few days passed. Kate said shit again. She misjudged her step when climbing into Scott's truck.

"Shit."

My eyes got big and I whipped my head at Scott. Scott's face morphed into father mode. I could feel his fury radiating off his body. He clutched the wheel.

*Oh shit. I should have warned her.*

"Kate! What did you just say?"

"Nothing."

Scott stepped out of the truck and slammed the driver's door. He walked to her side of the truck. I turned around and looked at Kate.

"Hey, Kate. Don't lie to your…"

Scott opened the door. "Look at me, Kate. YOU LOOK AT ME RIGHT NOW. Did you say shit? ANSWER! Did you say shit?"

Kate said nothing.

I looked at my hands in my lap. I could hear Emma trying to hold in laughter.

*Don't look at Emma. Don't look at Emma.*

"YOU ARE NEVER. EVER. TO SAY SHIT. Do you understand? Nod your head yes. You will be grounded all summer. Don't you say shit again."

Scott slammed the truck door shut. I looked back at Kate. She had fat tears in her eyes but they wouldn't fall.

"Kate, baby. Don't say that word, okay? Only when you're a grown-up."

Scott opened his door and started the truck. Kate never said the word shit again.

That's when I realized parenting books, teachers, child psychologists— they're all the same. They're working professionals. They won't tell parents to *nip that shit in the bud* because they respect parents. How do you stop a young child from cursing? You get in their face and yell, "Don't say shit again." That's how.

A six-year-old cursing is a phase. Kate didn't know what she was saying. She was copying me. This phase will come back in adulthood. I expect it. My daughters will grow up, become mothers, and call a Lego on the floor a piece of shit in front of their children.

I just hope they don't step on a Lego in front of their father.

*JULIE BURTON is a wife, mother, writer, outdoorswoman by marriage, K-State lover, and bacon hater living in Overland Park, Kansas. She is a columnist and contributing writer for* SIMPLYkc *magazine. She contributes to the blogs* Sammiches and Psych Meds *and* The Good Men Project. *She is a 2016-2017*

*National Geographic Kids ambassador. She is frequently named one of the* TODAY Show's *"Funniest Parents on Facebook" and* Babble, *courtesy of Disney's "Funniest Parents on Twitter."*

*And yes, she really does hate bacon. Please don't drop her as a friend.*

# They Grow Up So Fast and Stink So Much
## By Jen Mann
### *People I Want to Punch in the Throat*

Parents of littles, I'm going to say it and you're not going to like it: cherish this time; they grow up so fast. I know that if you're in the trenches of sticky hands and poopy diapers right now, you're thinking to yourself, "Nope. I'm out, you sanctimommy. Don't tell me to cherish this time. I'm exhausted, my boobs are leaking, I haven't showered in three days, and I have something I can't identify stuck in my hair and I don't even care. Sleep is a memory, food is whatever I can shove in my mouth before grubby hands snatch it from me, and sex…haha, sex…I don't even think I remember how to do it it's been so long. So, take your advice and shove it."

I know, I know. Barf. But hang on, just hear me out. Right now your kid still loves you. Yes, he smells like an outhouse and he leaves a sticky residue on everything he touches. He screams for attention and he demands breakfast before the sun is even up, but he also cuddles you and hugs you and gives you kisses. He snuggles in bed with you and says the sweetest things to you like, "Mommy, you're bootiful," when we all know you look like shit. Fast forward just ten years and the whole experience changes.

I don't even want to know what the sticky residue is that I find in his room now. He doesn't poop his pants anymore, but let's just say, I don't know what that boy is consuming, but my plumbing is suffering from his logs and I've invested heavily in plungers. He can get his own breakfast, but he leaves a wake of destruction throughout the entire kitchen: crusty cereal bowls, stale bread because he forgot to close the bag, and orange juice on the ceiling (don't ask how he did it, because he won't remember). The few times he ever asks to snuggle in my bed are weird and gross. He's as big as a small man and so he takes up a lot of room. He can't just nuzzle into your bosom anymore, so I half-hug him because he's an awkward man-child now and I'm acutely aware of how many times I think, "Is this appropriate? I don't have a bra on yet. I should just sleep in a bra from now on, on the off chance he decides to hop in bed with me." Just when I'm settling down and thinking, "Ahh, my baby is back. He wants to be with me," he lets one rip. An atomic burst that shakes the whole bed and literally heats up the sheets. Twelve-year-old boys' farts are the absolute worst. At least I think so. Probably sixteen-year-old boys' farts are even worse. I'll let you know when we get there. And it's not just his farts that stink. EVERYTHING stinks. And he's allergic to soap, water, and deodorant. But not Axe Body Spray.

When my kids were little, all of the parenting experts said, "Pick your battles. Pick your battles." And I did. The difference is, those battles were a little easier. When Baby Gomer was smelly, I could plop him in the tub and hose him down. Middle Grade Gomer, not so much. The child is as tall as me and probably stronger at this point. So when Middle Grade Gomer is ripe and I'm ready to battle over a bath, I have to get creative. At first, it was easy enough, because I could threaten to take away his Precious—his new phone. Precious never left his pocket, unless it was in his hand.

I could say, "Gomer, it's time to take a shower." And if he argued, I'd hold out my hand and demand Precious.

"Nooooo," he'd scream like the Wicked Witch of the West being threatened with a pail of soapy water. "Then get in the shower." He'd slink away and moments later I'd hear the water and I'd pat myself on the back for a job well done.

Then one day he got indifferent. "It's okay," he said. "You can have my phone. It's dead anyway. I'm not taking a shower."

I was a little shocked, but I didn't let on. You can't give middle schoolers even an ounce of superiority. They can live on that shit for weeks. "Okay, well, I'll keep it now, charge it up, and text all your friends that you smell like a homeless man's dirty ass crack." I held my breath, because I'd broken one of my Cardinal Parenting Rules: never make a promise you can't keep. For instance, when my kids were melting down in a restaurant or a store or the park or wherever and I'd say, "Keep this up and we're going home," I meant it. I was prepared to ask for a to-go box and eat my meal at home. I was ready to throw a screaming, tantrumming child over my shoulder and leave the mall, the park, or wherever. That's why I could never make a threat like that on an airplane. I could never say, "I'm going to tell the pilot to land this plane right now!" because then my kids would know I'm full of shit. Normally, I say what I mean. For instance, when Middle Grade Gomer wouldn't wear a coat when walking home in subzero temperatures because cool kids don't wear coats, I threatened to pull up in my minivan with ABBA blasting through my twelve premium speakers, wearing only pink bunny jammies and a coat, roll down the window and yell, "Hi, Wubbzy! Mommy forgot to give you your coat this morning. Here you go, pumpkin. Do you need Mommy to zip it for you or can you do it yourself now? Such a big boy! I know you wanted me to walk with you and hold your hand, but I just don't have the time today. Let's do it tomorrow! Love you sooooooo much!" THAT I could do, but I couldn't really text all of his friends. What was I thinking? I'd reached a breaking point. I was so sick of fighting with Gomer and having a smart-mouthed (smelly) kid sass me back, that the threat just slipped out. I was trying to figure out a way to reverse it when I saw the look on his face.

OHMAGAHD. He turned green. He broke out in a light sheen of sweat and his eyes grew wide and fearful. He believed my crazy shit. "You'd really do that, wouldn't you?" he demanded.

"Try me," I said, staring him down. *Ha! I'm a parenting genius!* I thought. *And I didn't even have to lie.* Let me just interject here and say that I'm not afraid to lie to my kids. Yes, I know it's kind of confusing. I mean what I say when I threaten an action, but I can bullshit all day long. There's a difference. Lying to my kids is one of the staples in my parenting tips and tricks. I know a lot of you just clutched your pearls and swooned. But come on, it's one of the few perks we get as parents. Plus, we're already lying to them now. We lie to them all the time. "If you don't hold my hand in a store, you will get lost." Really? Do you see a lot of stories on the nightly news talking about toddlers who have become lost due to lack of hand-holding? Of course there are a few terrifying stories of children getting hurt or dying after wandering off, but the chances your child will fall down a well in the middle of Target are pretty low. We lie about Santa and the Easter Bunny and the Tooth Fairy. "Knock it off, Santa is watching! Yeah, he watches in July." We lie about dead animals by the side of the road. "I'm pretty sure that deer was sleeping. Yes, even without his head he can still sleep. He's fine." We lie about sex. "Where do babies come from? Um, storks and cabbage patches, mostly. Who wants chocolate?" We lie about the ice cream truck. "Sorry, kids, it only plays music when the ice cream is sold out." What? Is that one just me? Doesn't everyone use that ice cream truck lie? Well, you should; it will save you thousands of dollars on Bomb Pops. You're welcome.

"I hate showers," he whined.

"Gomer," I said softly. "Go upstairs and get in the shower and wash your hair. In fact, wash everything twice. I don't trust that any of it will be done properly."

"Whyyyyy?" he moaned. "I'm just going to get sweaty and smelly again tomorrow."

I nodded. "Yes, that is correct. We bathe every day because every day we stink."

"You don't shower every day," he argued. "Some days you don't even get dressed."

I hate when your kids use your own logic against you. "I spend my day sitting at a desk. I'm not working up a sweat like you are. And most nights I shower before bed, you just aren't around to see that. Besides, this is about you, not me. I'm the adult. I can do what I like. You are the child and you must bathe."

"No," he said stubbornly. "I don't even smell that bad."

I was at a loss. I couldn't physically remove him to the shower. He moved to sit on the couch. "Don't sit there," I ordered.

"What?"

"You smell and I don't want my couch to stink. You may not sit on the couch if you haven't showered and washed your hair."

He moved to the rug.

"Nope, not there either; you'll make the rug smell."

"Fine, I'll go to my room!" he said.

"No. I own everything in that room and I will not have it ruined by your funk. You can have one square of hardwood floor to sit on."

"But where will I sleep?" he asked.

"You'll sleep on your patch of hardwood floor," I said and I meant it. Sleeping on the floor for one night would cure his smelly ass.

"Sometimes you really suck," Gomer said, stomping up the stairs to the horrible shower with plenty of hot water, fluffy towels, and Old Spice soap and shampoo. (That kid should thank me, actually; my mom made my brother use the same flowery soaps and shampoos we used. When my brother lost his shower battles with my mom, he came out smelling like roses and strawberries. At least I brought my son "manly"-scented shit! He should kiss my feet!)

"Yes, I do, dear. Please make sure you get the shower curtain INSIDE of the shower this time. The baseboards are starting to warp from the flooding you're causing every time you pretend to shower."

This threat kept him in line for a few weeks but then he found a way around it. I should have known he was up to no good, because he'd actually gone to the shower willingly. He'd been skateboarding and when he came inside, everything was soaked through with sweat. "You need—" I started.

"Yeah, yeah, I need a shower. I know," Gomer agreed. He headed up the stairs. No stomping, no arguing about how his life would be ruined by hot water.

I smiled and my smug ass thought, *And now I've won the war.*

A few minutes later he returned. He was wearing clean clothes and his hair was damp, but…something was off. He didn't smell terrific and there was something about his hair…I took a closer look. "Gomer, did you wash your hair?" I asked.

"Yeah," he said, barely looking up from Precious.

"How did you wash your hair but now it's partially dry?"

His head snapped up. "What?"

"Your hair is dry on the ends. It's only wet at the roots. How did you manage this?"

"Oh, uh, I blow-dried it," he said with the shiftiest of eyes. Lucky for me, Gomer is a horrible liar.

"Gomer!" I screeched. "Why are you lying to me? Why is it a battle to get you in the shower and get you washed properly? What is the problem?"

Gomer had the decency to look chagrined, but he wasn't budging. He just sat there and stared at me. It was a face-off. I looked at his phone. Was I really going to text all his friends and say he smells like a homeless man's dirty ass crack? I wracked my brain. I had to threaten him with something I could actually follow through on, because this was going to be a battle to the death. I was going to have to follow through with my threat.

"Fine," I said. "Your phone is off-limits for a week and you'll still take shower. Wait here, please. I'm going to get my swimsuit on."

"What?!"

"I'm going to put on my swimsuit and then I'm going to sit on top of you and wrangle you out of your clothes—you might be stronger than me, but I still outweigh you. I'm going to drag you into my shower and I'm going to scrub you down with the toilet brush and soap. I just need to get on my swimsuit. I don't want to get my clothes wet."

"Mom, stop. You're not going to do that," he said.

"Oh, I am," I said, in my softest, deadliest voice.

All it took was me opening the drawer where I keep my swimsuits. Gomer heard the familiar squeal of the wood and he screamed, "I'm going now! I'm going! God, stop, Mom! Stop! I'm going!"

I listened to his man-size feet scramble up my stairs and I sighed heavily with relief. *That was close*, I thought. He had no idea, I was ready to fulfill my threat, but it would have been worse for me than him, because me in a swimsuit is actually more embarrassing than him being scrubbed with a toilet brush.

*JEN MANN is best known for her wildly popular and hysterical blog* People I Want to Punch in the Throat. *She has been described by many as Erma Bombeck—with f-bombs. Jen is known for her hilarious rants and funny observations on everything from parenting to gift-giving to celebrity behavior to politics to Elves on Shelves. She does not suffer fools lightly. Jen is the author of the* New York Times *bestseller* People I Want to Punch in the Throat: Competitive Crafters, Drop-Off Despots, and Other Suburban Scourges, *which was a Finalist for a Goodreads Reader's Choice Award. Her latest book is a YA fiction book called* My Lame Life. *She is also the mastermind behind the* New York Times *bestselling* I Just Want to Pee Alone *series.*

*Jen is a married mother of two children whom she calls Gomer and Adolpha in her writings—she swears their real names are actually worse.*

# NOTES FROM THE EDITOR

Thank you for reading this collection of essays. We appreciate your support and we hope you enjoyed it. We also hope you will tell a friend—or thirty about this. Please do us a huge favor and leave us a review.

# OTHER BOOKS AVAILABLE

*My Lame Life*

*People I Want to Punch in the Throat: Competitive Crafters, Drop Off Despots, and Other Suburban Scourges*

*Spending the Holidays with People I Want to Punch in the Throat*

*I Just Want to Be Perfect*

*I STILL Just Want to Pee Alone*

*I Just Want to Be Alone*

*I Just Want to Pee Alone*

## OTHER SINGLES AVAILABLE

*Just a Few People I Want to Punch in the Throat (Vol. 1)*
*Just a Few People I Want to Punch in the Throat (Vol. 2)*
*Just A Few People I Want to Punch in the Throat (Vol. 3)*
*Just a Few People I Want to Punch in the Throat (Vol. 4)*
*Just a Few People I Want to Punch in the Throat (Vol. 5)*

Made in the USA
Monee, IL
07 February 2020